For Keely, Cailín, and Brendan

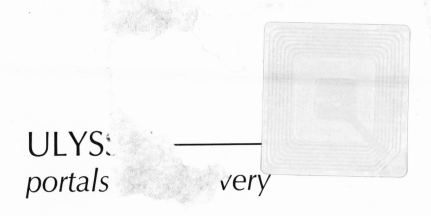

ULYS:

portals *very*

TWAYNE'S MASTERWORK STUDIES
Robert Lecker, General Editor

ULYSSES——
portals of discovery

Patrick A. McCarthy

TWAYNE PUBLISHERS • Boston
A Division of G.K. Hall & Co.

Ulysses: portals of discovery

Twayne's Masterwork Studies No. 41

Copyright 1990 by G. K. Hall & Co.
All rights reserved.
Published by Twayne Publishers
A Division of G. K. Hall & Co.
70 Lincoln Street
Boston, Massachusetts 02111

Copyediting supervised by Barbara Sutton
Book production by Patricia D'Agostino

Typeset in 10/14 sabon
by Huron Valley Graphics Inc.

Printed on permanent/durable acid-free paper
and bound in the United States of America

Library of Congress Cataloging-in-Publication Data

McCarthy, Patrick A., 1945–
    Ulysses—portals of discovery / Patrick A. McCarthy.
        p.   cm.—(Twayne's masterwork studies ; no. 4)
    Includes bibliographical references.
    ISBN 0-8057-7976-0 (alk. paper).—ISBN 0-8057-8026-2 (pbk. :
alk. paper)
    1. Joyce, James, 1882–1941. Ulysses. I. Title. II. Series.
PR6019.09U6835   1990
823'.912—dc20   89-15566
                                                                CIP

Why don't you write sensible books that people can understand?

—Nora to James Joyce

More interesting if you understood what it was all about.

—Leopold Bloom

John Eglinton looked in the tangled glowworm of his lamp.

—The world believes that Shakespeare made a mistake, he said, and got out of it as quickly and as best he could.

—Bosh! Stephen said rudely. A man of genius makes no mistakes. His errors are volitional and are the portals of discovery.

Contents

Note on the References and Acknowledgments
Preface
Chronology: James Joyce's Life and Works

1. Historical Context	1
2. The Importance of the Work	9
3. Critical Reception	14

A Reading

4. Arrangements of Reality	25
5. A Comedy of Errors	36
6. Dublin Alligators	52
7. An Epic of Two Races	68
8. Reading in Ulysses	94

Appendix: An Outline of Ulysses	113
Notes	126
Bibliography	134
Index	139
About the Author	145

Note on the References and Acknowledgments

Throughout this study, I have used as my text the 1986 Random House edition of *Ulysses*. Based on the "reading text" in the three-volume Garland *Ulysses*, this edition is at present the one most readily available to American readers, and its correction of innumerable printer's errors represents a substantial improvement over previous American texts (the 1934 and 1961 Random House editions). Since many readers still use the 1961 Random House text, however, I have keyed citations to both the 1986 and the 1961 edition. Parenthetical citations refer, first, to episode and line numbers for the 1986 text, and then, page numbers for the 1961 edition. For example, (14.160/387) refers to line 160 of the fourteenth episode (Oxen of the Sun) in the 1986 text, which corresponds to page 387 in the 1961 Random House edition.

References to Joyce's other works, to his letters, to Richard Ellmann's biography of Joyce (cited as "Ellmann"), and to the articles and reviews included in *James Joyce: The Critical Heritage*, edited by Robert H. Deming (cited as "Deming"), are included parenthetically in the text. In each case I have quoted or referred to the current edition listed in the Bibliography.

A segment of chapter 7 is a slightly modified version of a note that appeared in the Winter 1984 issue of the *James Joyce Quarterly* under the title "The Case of Reuben J. Dodd." I am grateful to the *James Joyce Quarterly* for permission to include this material in the present book.

Patrick Donovan, whose silverpoint drawing of Joyce serves as the frontispiece to this volume, is a retired police officer who now lives in Port Richie, Florida. Silverpoint—the art of drawing with a silver stylus on specially prepared paper—is a Renaissance technique practiced by only a few artists today. Mr. Donovan's silverpoint portrait of D. H. Lawrence is the frontispiece for *"Sons and Lovers": A Novel of Division and Desire* by Ross C Murfin (Twayne's Masterwork Studies, 1987), and his silverpoint drawings of T. S. Eliot and Samuel Beckett have appeared in *The Carrell: Journal of the Friends of the University of Miami Library.*

In writing this book I have incurred many debts, especially to the scholars cited in the Notes and Bibliography (including those with whom I disagree) and to my colleagues and students at the University of Miami. My greatest debt is to Zack Bowen—chairman, colleague, and friend—whose support and encouragement made completion of this book possible.

Preface

The present study of *Ulysses* derives from one of the central motifs of Joyce's fiction: the encounter. Gerald Bruns has remarked that while "the basic unit of Joyce's fiction is the encounter," it is generally the case that "the encounter does not, on the whole, amount to very much; that is, Joyce's encounters are intrinsically ironic, because our expectations of dramatic confrontations are almost never fulfilled."[1] Both the *Odyssey* and the *Divine Comedy* depend upon a series of encounters that lead either to recognition or to a failure to recognize identity, so *Ulysses* has distinguished antecedents in its reliance on the encounter. Joyce's encounters, however, are typically self-encounters: as Bruns notes, Bloom's "Think you're escaping and run into yourself" (13.1110/377) and Stephen's belief that life consists of "meeting ourselves" (9.1046/213) encapsulate the mode of the Joycean encounter.[2] Thus it is unsurprising to discover that the *Dubliners* story "An Encounter" culminates in a moment of self-recognition: "My voice had an accent of forced bravery in it and I was ashamed of my paltry stratagem. I had to call the name again before Mahony saw me and hallooed in answer. How my heart beat as he came running across the field to me! He ran as if to bring me aid. And I was penitent; for in my heart I had always despised him a little" (28).

The central encounter in *Ulysses*, I believe, is the reader's encounter with the text itself, and with the facts, values, interpretations, and judgments presented therein. Within Joyce's novel, encounters may take many forms: characters may meet (or avoid meeting) other characters; they encounter the newspapers, books, flyers, and other texts that they read; they try to separate truth from fiction. My discussion, therefore, considers various forms of encountering as they apply to the reader's discovery of *Ulysses*. In sketching the book's historical context I discuss the forces that Joyce encountered, and attempted to master, as he conceived his epic novel. In a brief consideration of the book's importance I emphasize the ways in which it has influenced the modern novel. The survey of critical perspectives is intended to give an overview of various ways that different critics have responded to their encounters with *Ulysses*. In the following chapters I note, first, the ways in which the book demands a constantly shifting response to its styles and perspectives; then, the roles that errors, misunderstandings, and rumors play in *Ulysses;* next, the troubling and complex question of ethnic and national identity, which helps to shape not only the characters' response to other characters but our response as well; and finally, the way in which our encounters with *Ulysses* are mirrored by a text that continually gives us examples of characters reading other texts. Ultimately, I will suggest, Joyce's readers encounter themselves, so that their various encounters with *Ulysses* serve as portals of self-discovery.

James Joyce
Portrait by Patrick Donovan, 1988

Chronology: James Joyce's Life and Works

1882	James Augustine Joyce, first surviving child of John Stanislaus Joyce and Mary Jane Murray Joyce, is born 2 February at 41 Brighton Square in Rathgar, a suburb south of Dublin. (Nine other children would survive infancy, including his brother John Stanislaus ["Stannie"], born 17 December 1884.)
1887	Joyces move to 1 Martello Terrace in Bray, a more expensive suburb on the coast.
1888	Joyce is sent to Clongowes Wood College, a Jesuit boarding school in County Kildare.
1891	Withdrawn from Clongowes due to his father's financial decline, Joyce goes for two years to a Christian Brothers school in Dublin. Charles Stewart Parnell dies 6 October; nine-year-old Joyce composes a now-lost poem, "Et Tu, Healy," angrily denouncing Parnell's "betrayal" by his former supporters.
1892–1893	Joyces move to Blackrock, then to Dublin; Joyce enters Belvedere College, a Jesuit school, in April 1893.
1898	Joyce enrolls at the Royal University in Dublin (now University College, Dublin).
1900	Joyce reads a paper, "Drama and Life," at a meeting of the Literary and Historical Society of the university and publishes "Ibsen's New Drama," a review of *When We Dead Awaken*.
1901	"The Day of the Rabblement," Joyce's essay attacking the Irish Literary Theatre (antecedent of the Abbey Theatre), is privately printed.
1902	Joyce reads his paper on James Clarence Mangan before the literary society, later publishing it in *St. Stephen's*, the college literary journal that had rejected "The Day of the Rabblement." In October he graduates from the university with a B.A. in modern languages; in December he leaves for Paris, supposedly to study medicine.

1903	In April, Joyce is recalled from Paris by a telegram reading (according to *Ulysses*) "Nother dying come home father." Mother dies of cancer in August.
1904	Joyce remains in Dublin (living briefly with Oliver St. John Gogarty—"Buck" Mulligan in *Ulysses*—at the Martello Tower in Sandycove) until 8 October, when he leaves Dublin for the continent in the company of Nora Barnacle, a young Galway woman whom he met in June. In Dublin, he writes "A Portrait, of the Artist" (essay); begins *Stephen Hero*, the earlier version of *A Portrait of the Artist as a Young Man*; and publishes, in the *Irish Homestead*, three *Dubliners* stories: "The Sisters," "Eveline," and "After the Race." On the continent, Joyce and Nora go first to Zurich, where an expected job falls through, and then to Pola, where he teaches at the Berlitz school.
1905	Joyce moves to Trieste and teaches at the Berlitz school; in July, Nora gives birth to their first child, Giorgio. In October, Stanislaus comes to live with them in Trieste. Joyce satirizes the Irish Literary Revival in his poem "The Holy Office," privately printed in Trieste. He completes twelve *Dubliners* stories and submits the manuscript to Grant Richards.
1906	Grant Richards accepts *Dubliners* for publication, then (after Joyce sends two more stories for the collection) requests numerous changes and eventually rejects the book. From July 1906 to March 1907 Joyce works at a bank in Rome.
1907	Returning to Trieste in March, Joyce completes "The Dead," the final story of *Dubliners,* and begins to revise *Stephen Hero* as *A Portrait of the Artist as a Young Man*. Elkin Mathews publishes *Chamber Music*, a volume of poems. Joyce's daughter, Lucia, is born in July.
1909–1912	Joyce visits Ireland twice in 1909 and arranges for Maunsel and Co. to publish *Dubliners*. Although Joyce corrects proofs in 1910, the publisher requests extensive changes. In 1912 trip to Ireland to rescue the collection fails; Maunsel refuses to honor its agreement, and Joyce writes his broadside "Gas from a Burner" in retaliation.
1914	Grant Richards agrees to honor the 1906 contract and publishes *Dubliners;* Dora Marsden begins serialization of *A Portrait* in the *Egoist* before Joyce writes the last chapter. Joyce begins writing *Exiles* and planning *Ulysses*.
1915	Joyce moves his family to Zurich for the duration of the war.
1916	*A Portrait* is published.

Chronology: James Joyce's Life and Works

1917	Despite undergoing his first eye operation, for glaucoma (numerous other eye operations would follow during the remainder of his life), Joyce completes the first three chapters of *Ulysses*. Harriet Shaw Weaver begins sending Joyce money, at first in the form of anonymous gifts.
1918	Serialization of *Ulysses* begins in the *Little Review*, continuing until late 1920, when the New York Society for the Suppression of Vice succeeds in having *Ulysses* declared obscene and banned from the United States. *Exiles* is published.
1919	After the war, Joyce returns to Trieste.
1920	Joyce moves to Paris, his last major move until 1940.
1922	*Ulysses* is published on 2 February in honor of Joyce's birthday.
1923	Joyce begins *Finnegans Wake*, whose title he reveals only to Nora.
1924	The first fragment of *Work in Progress*, the working title for *Finnegans Wake*, is published. Other publications in 1924 include the first French translation of *A Portrait* and Herbert Gorman's *James Joyce: His First Forty Years*, the first full-length study of Joyce's work.
1927	A petition signed by 167 writers and intellectuals, including Benedetto Croce, Albert Einstein, Virginia Woolf, and W. B. Yeats, protests Samuel Roth's unauthorized publication of *Ulysses*. *Pomes Penyeach*, Joyce's second collection of poems, is published.
1929	Twelve essays on *Work in Progress* (*Finnegans Wake*) appear under the title *Our Exagmination round his Factification for Incamination of Work in Progress*.
1930	*James Joyce's "Ulysses": A Study* by Stuart Gilbert—the first significant book-length study of *Ulysses*—is published.
1931	Joyce and Nora are married ("for testamentary reasons") in July; Joyce's father dies in December.
1932	"Ecce Puer," one of Joyce's most moving poems, is occasioned by his father's death in December 1931 and his grandson Stephen's birth in February 1932. Lucia Joyce has a mental breakdown (the diagnosis would be schizophrenia); she will spend most of the last fifty years of her life in asylums.
1933	Judge John M. Woolsey rules that *Ulysses* is not pornographic and "may, therefore, be admitted into the United States."
1934	*Ulysses* is published in the United States; Joyce's Zurich friend Frank Budgen publishes *James Joyce and the Making of "Ulysses."*

1936	Joyce's *Collected Poems,* containing *Chamber Music, Pomes Penyeach,* and "Ecce Puer," are published.
1939	*Finnegans Wake* is published, the first copy appearing on Joyce's birthday.
1940	Herbert Gorman's *James Joyce,* the first full-length biography of Joyce, is published. Joyce and Nora leave France for Zurich; Lucia remains in an asylum in Vichy France.
1941	Joyce dies 13 January in Zurich.

Historical Context

Haines detached from his underlip some fibres of tobacco before he spoke.
—I can quite understand that, he said calmly. An Irishman must think like that, I daresay. We feel in England that we have treated you rather unfairly. It seems history is to blame. (1.645–49 / 20)

Many of the twentieth century's most important writers have been literally displaced people, political or cultural exiles who have spent most of their literary lives outside their native countries: writers as different in other respects as Joseph Conrad, Gertrude Stein, Ezra Pound, T. S. Eliot, and Vladimir Nabokov are familiar examples. In Ireland, the phenomenon occurs with particular frequency: Oscar Wilde, George Bernard Shaw, Sean O'Casey, and Samuel Beckett are among the more significant Irish writers of the past century who have written the bulk of their works outside Ireland. This sense of displacement is especially acute in the case of James Joyce, who was born, raised, and educated in Dublin, but spent almost all of his adult life on the continent, where he imaginatively re-created the city he had left.

Significantly, the wandering, "exiled" writer portrayed, in *Ulys-*

ses, a protagonist whose wanderings about Dublin and consciousness of his marginal place in Irish society reflect Joyce's own situation. Leopold Bloom's cultural displacement is reflected in his simultaneous roles as a twentieth-century Irishman, the son of a Hungarian Jew, and, symbolically, the reincarnation of the ancient Greek hero whose name, in its Latin form, serves as the book's title. Dominic Manganiello has noted that in *Ulysses* we see the culmination of "Joyce's hopes for the spiritual liberation of his country,"[1] to which we might add that in assigning the role of hero to a "competent keyless citizen" (17.1019/697) who represents none of the groups contending for power in Dublin 1904, Joyce demonstrated his rejection of what Bloom would call "force, hatred, history, all that" (12.1481/333). To awaken from the "nightmare" of history is the dream of Stephen Dedalus (2.377/34); to redeem Ireland from that nightmare was one of Joyce's goals in *Ulysses*. Thus it is important to understand the historical context in which Joyce conceived and wrote *Ulysses*.

In 1922, the year in which *Ulysses* was published, Ireland became largely independent of Great Britain through the founding of the Irish Free State (six northeastern counties were partitioned off to form the separate state of Northern Ireland). By this time, however, Joyce had been away from Ireland for nearly two decades, and the Ireland of his imagination was the one in which he had lived between 1882 and 1904. For Joyce, as for his father, the major Irish political hero of this period was Charles Stewart Parnell (1846–91), who was first elected to the British Parliament in 1875 and became the leader of the Home Rule party. In 1890, Parnell's adulterous affair with Kitty O'Shea led to his being named corespondent in the divorce case filed by her husband, a member of Parliament from Parnell's party, and pressure from the British press and the Catholic Church resulted in Parnell's removal from the party leadership. The following October Parnell died, and Joyce's father bitterly denounced those who had deserted "the Chief" in his hour of need. In the Joyce household, Christmas dinner was spoiled by the violent quarrel described in the first chapter of *A Portrait of the Artist as a Young Man*.

For Joyce, the triumph of petty-minded moralism over the idealism and self-sacrifice of Parnell was a warning that Ireland posed dangers to other forces of liberation, including those of literary art. In 1899 Joyce attended a production of William Butler Yeats's play *The Countess Cathleen* and refused to sign a petition condemning it for what some other university students regarded as heretical and anti-Irish elements. Despite his admiration for this play, however, Joyce deeply distrusted the Irish Literary Revival of the late nineteenth and early twentieth centuries, a movement born out of the desire to resurrect a distinct Irish cultural identity through literary and dramatic works on Irish subjects written in the English language. A confirmed urbanite, Joyce felt no sense of kinship with the Literary Revivalists' emphasis on the Irish heroic past and on the importance of the Irish peasantry. Joyce's distaste for the Literary Revival surfaced in two early works: a broadside entitled "The Day of the Rabblement" (1901), which attacked the Irish Literary Theatre's provincialism and its apparent willingness to compromise its ideals to gain popular support, and "The Holy Office" (1905), a satiric poem in which Joyce lampooned contemporary Irish writers, portraying them as unworldly aesthetes whose "dreamy dreams" overlook the "filthy streams" of real life.

That literature should portray life as it is, rather than as we might hope it to be, was an attitude Joyce derived more from continental writers than from their Irish counterparts. Flaubert, Tolstoy, and Ibsen were among the authors Joyce most admired for their candid and courageous treatment of their subjects as well as for their consummate artistry. The influence of nineteenth-century realism and naturalism can be seen clearly in the fifteen stories of Joyce's *Dubliners*, where the characters' entrapment by their urban environment, by a repressive political and religious atmosphere, and by their own inadequacies produces the stagnation and frustration that Joyce called "paralysis." The purpose of the book, Joyce told his publisher, was to give his countrymen "one good look at themselves in my nicely polished looking-glass" (*Letters* 1:64). That look proved sufficiently unflattering to deter the Irish publishing house of Maunsel and Co. from living up to its agreement to publish the book, and it was only after a decade of wrangling with publishers that *Dubliners* was finally published by the English firm of Grant Richards.

If *Dubliners* portrays the city of Joyce's youth as something to escape, *A Portrait of the Artist as a Young Man* chronicles the events leading up to Joyce's own escape. In the *Portrait*, Stephen Dedalus, Joyce's autobiographical protagonist, struggles against the "nets" of "nationality, language, religion," regarding Ireland as a devouring mother, "the old sow that eats her farrow" (203). At the outset of the novel, Stephen is seen within the environment of his family, and Joyce records Stephen's impressions ("When you wet the bed first it is warm then it gets cold") and his attempts to understand the principles of order within his world ("Uncle Charles and Dante clapped. They were older than his father and mother but uncle Charles was older than Dante" [7]). By the end of *Portrait*, however, Stephen has begun to control his environment, as our view of Dublin is mediated by Stephen's diary. Even so, the book's conclusion is susceptible to ironic readings: Stephen's grand declaration that he will "forge in the smithy of my soul the uncreated conscience of my race" is consistent with Joyce's belief that modern writers must create the "conscience" of their nation, but this seems too large a task for the twenty-year-old diarist who has noted, in the same entry, that his flight from the stifling environment of the mother country is aided by his mother, who "is putting my new secondhand clothes in order" (252–53).

The *Portrait* records and reinterprets Joyce's life up to spring 1902. At the end of that year, Joyce took his B.A. in modern languages from the National University and left for Paris, where he made a half-hearted attempt to study medicine and then devoted himself to writing reviews and occasional pieces and to reading at the Bibliothèque Nationale and the Bibliothèque Sainte-Geneviève. Within a few months he was recalled to Dublin by a telegram from his father that said his mother was dying. The death of his mother in August 1903 removed his principal reason for remaining in Dublin, yet he stayed on for more than a year, publishing three *Dubliners* stories in the *Irish Homestead* and beginning the book that would evolve into the *Portrait*. When he left Ireland in October 1904 he was accompanied by Nora Barnacle, a young Galway woman he had met in June.

In 1906, while working as a bank clerk in Rome, Joyce conceived *Ulysses* as a short story for *Dubliners*. Joyce abandoned the idea of writing the story for inclusion in *Dubliners* but retained his interest in the figure of the charitable cuckold, and in 1914, while staying in Trieste, he began the work that would take him the next seven years to complete. At the heart of *Ulysses* is the meeting of Stephen Dedalus and Leopold Bloom: youthful egotism and mature compassion, a would-be exile and the son of an immigrant, representatives, as *Ulysses* tells us, of the "artistic" and "scientific" temperaments (17.559–60/683). In a broad sense, Stephen is a version of Joyce's youth and Bloom of his maturity, and the fact that Joyce chose to represent himself as a pair of outsiders indicates his continuing alienation from the city in which he was raised. In arranging an encounter between two aspects of his own life and character, placing side by side two figures who represent him in different phases of his life, Joyce gives us one example of the book's parallactic technique: we see Dublin through Bloom's eyes and Stephen's (and eventually through Molly's as well), and while each viewpoint is limited, the juxtaposition of various perspectives hints at the larger, fully human, viewpoint toward which *Ulysses* reaches. Moreover, since the book continually demonstrates the inadequacy of traditional novelistic characterization to account for the connections between people, Joyce appears to be arguing that Stephen, Bloom, and the other characters are part of a greater reality that transcends individual identity; in peppering his book with a wide range of literary allusions, entitling it *Ulysses*, and forging a parallel with one of the central myths of Western society, Joyce suggests that the reality of which Stephen and Bloom are part is not merely historical but imaginative. He also implies that the "race" whose "conscience" Stephen vowed to create might well be the human race.

In the opening chapter of *Ulysses*, Buck Mulligan challenges Stephen to work with him to "Hellenise" Ireland (1.158/7). The

alert reader will note the frequency with which the Greek theme
surfaces in *Ulysses*, from the Greek word *Chrysostomos* ("Golden-
mouthed"), which describes both Mulligan's oratorical style and the
condition of his teeth (1.26/3), to Molly Bloom's fortuitous references to Ulysses (18.682/757), Calypso (18.837/761), and Europa
(18.849/761, 18.1337/775). Molly, of course, has no intention of
providing us with classical allusions: her Ulysses is President Grant,
who visited Gibraltar when Molly was a girl; H M S Calypso was a
ship on which her first suitor, Harry Mulvey, sailed; and Europa ·
Point is at the southern tip of Gibraltar. These allusions have their
larger significance for us rather than for the characters, who are
unaware that they are living in a "Hellenised" Dublin. Nonetheless,
it is worth noting that the artistic transfiguration of Dublin accom-
plished in *Ulysses* sets Joyce's aims apart from those of the three
major groups that challenged British political and cultural hegemony
in early twentieth-century Ireland: the Irish nationalists, the Gaelic
language revivalists, and the Dublin literary establishment.

The nationalists' willingness to resort to violence to achieve their
aims, the Gaelic Leaguers' attempt to resuscitate what for Joyce was a
dead language, and the Literary Revivalists' contempt for the urban
middle class all, in Joyce's view, derived from narrow or parochial views
of a world that needed to be experienced from every possible angle, in
order to explore its great variety and richness. In his famous 1892
lecture "The Necessity for De-Anglicising Ireland," which stressed the
importance of reviving the Irish language as a vital factor in Irish life,
Douglas Hyde had set forth the twin parallels of the Irish with the
Greeks and the Jews: "Just when we should be starting to build up anew
the Irish race and the Gaelic nation—as within our own recollection
Greece has been built up anew—we find ourselves despoiled of the
bricks of nationality" through the loss of the Irish language. If the
language were revived, Hyde said, it would be just as "disgraceful for an
educated Irishman . . . to be ignorant of his own language . . . as for an
educated Jew to be quite ignorant of Hebrew."[2] Joyce's own prescrip-
tion for Ireland had to do with dragging it into the modern world, de-
Anglicizing it not in order to return to the Celtic past but to bring it into

the mainstream of European culture as an equal partner; his parallels with Greek and Jewish literature are not merely a conventional means of conferring respect on the Irish but a device for suggesting that a narrowly racial or nationalistic view of Irish events was inadequate. In any event, if the Dublin of *Ulysses* is not thoroughly de-Anglicized, it is Hellenized in a way that Buck Mulligan likely would not recognize, and the book in turn is a device for Celticizing modern English literature.

In 1918 Joyce told Georges Borach that "As an artist I am against every state. . . . The state is concentric, man is eccentric. Thence arises an eternal struggle. The monk, the bachelor, and the anarchist are in the same category" (Ellmann 446). Joyce's preference for the eccentric over the concentric, the human over the mechanical, is evident throughout *Ulysses,* where Bloom's fallibility becomes one of the qualities through which he humanizes the world in which he exists. In *Finnegans Wake* (1939), Joyce's last and most complex book, we can see the same distaste for political conformity and fanaticism that Bloom expresses in *Ulysses.* Events both in Ireland and on the continent—the Irish Civil War between Free Staters and die-hard Republicans on the one hand, the rise of totalitarianism on the other—confirmed Joyce's distrust of politics and history and his belief that literature should aim at creating a broader, more complete, vision of humanity than modern political movements are wont to do. In the *Wake,* Joyce challenges racial and national boundaries by producing a composite, multilevel, universal history. The very language of *Finnegans Wake,* which blends, distorts, and creates words to suit Joyce's purposes (rather than aligning those purposes to a pre-existing language), constitutes an answer to those who would seek a single meaning in any event, historical or otherwise. Indeed, as Seamus Deane observes, Joyce hoped to develop a language that "would extend the range of possible signification to an ultimate degree of openness, thereby setting itself against the closed world of limited and limiting historical fact."[3]

The development of that language, in *Ulysses,* entailed several activities. First, there is the abolition of a single privileged perspective and the substitution for the omniscient narrator of a series of alternative viewpoints. Second, Joyce treats error, misunderstanding, and rumor not merely as deviations from the truth but as alternative forms of reality, as round pegs of human error that refuse to fit into the square hole of the mechanical world. Third, he satirizes racial and ethnic stereotyping as well as the rhetoric of Irish nationalism. And finally, he presents us with an ironic portrayal of ourselves as error-prone readers who manage despite our inadequacies to arrive at a version of the truth. In the critical reading that follows these introductory chapters, I will focus on these Joycean encounters between the world and the human imagination.

The Importance
of the Work

When the American musician Arthur Laubenstein confessed to Joyce his inability to understand *Ulysses,* Joyce told him that "the value of the book is its new style" (Ellmann 557). Joyce was being uncharacteristically modest in claiming only one area of importance, but it is generally true that the influence of *Ulysses* on the modern novel has depended less on what the book means than on how it generates its meaning. Among Joyce's most influential innovations are those involving the abandonment of traditional omniscient narration for a more direct representation of a character's mental processes, the use of several distinct styles within the narrative, the occasional abandonment of the narrative proper for exercises in fantasy or parody, the extensive use of literary allusions or correspondences, and the book's generally reflexive or self-referential nature—its tendency to demonstrate openly its status as a literary artifact and to treat its language and techniques not merely as vehicles for the expression of meaning, but as one of the book's subjects.

One way in which *Ulysses* has influenced subsequent novels is through its reliance on interior monologue, or the nonnarrated thoughts of a character, and on stream-of-consciousness style. Both of these narrative strategies involve a relatively direct encounter with a character's mental processes: interior monologue plunges us directly into a character's thoughts, without the mediating presence of a narrator, while stream-of-consciousness presents those thoughts to us as a series of half-formed ideas linked by a process of association. In essence, both in style (stream-of-consciousness) and in narrative perspective (interior monologue), Joyce presents us with thoughts in process, carrying us through the fluctuations of the character's mind rather than interpreting that mind for us.

Joyce gives us several distinct examples of stream-of-consciousness writing, for at various times, the book focuses on the minds of Stephen, Bloom, and Molly, each of which is distinguished from the others by subject matter, diction, syntax, and rhythm. These are far from the book's only styles, however, for *Ulysses* might almost be regarded as an encyclopedia of styles and perspectives. The stylistic differences among the early chapters are relatively subtle compared to those between the extravagant dramatic form of Circe and the meandering, cliché-ridden language of Eumaeus or the catechistic assurances of Ithaca. One of the cornerstones of modernist writing is the belief that form and content are essentially inseparable, that—as Samuel Beckett put it in his monograph on Proust—form is a "concretion" of content, "the revelation of a world."[1] In *Ulysses* Joyce attempted to fit language and situation to one another, as, for example, in the extensive use of rhetorical figures in Aeolus to suggest one of the stylistic features of Victorian and Edwardian journalism, or the dependence on musical motifs in Sirens. Joyce's styles in the later episodes, however, tend more to the parodic than to the representational, and in general there is an ironic distance between the apparent claims of a style and its effect on the reader: thus the manner of Ithaca strives for empirical certainty but succeeds only in mocking its own pretense of objectivity.

The most fantastic of the parodies may be in the Cyclops and Circe episodes, in sections that stand apart from the main narrative line of *Ulysses*. The first-person narrative of Cyclops is interrupted for a description of the Citizen—in actual fact, a cadger of drinks and a jingoistic blowhard—as "a broadshouldered deepchested stronglimbed frank-eyed redhaired freelyfreckled shaggybearded widemouthed largenosed longheaded deepvoiced barekneed brawnyhanded hairylegged ruddy-faced sinewyarmed hero" (12.152–55/296). The parodic description of the "hero" takes on a life of its own, culminating in the list of "Irish heroes and heroines of antiquity" whose "tribal images" hang from the giant's belt. Here, the inflated language has the effect of deflating what it describes, all the more so since the list of "Irish heroes" includes such unlikely candidates as Julius Caesar, Captain Nemo, and Herodotus. Moreover, there is an effect akin to the sense of "alienation" or strangeness (*Verfremdung*) that Bertolt Brecht sought in his plays, for the departure from the primary or "literal" level of narration serves as a reminder that art is not reality but only an attempt to capture some aspect of the real. The relationship of the realistic and the fantastic is even more complex in Circe, where most of the chapter consists of a series of expressionistic fantasies whose relationship to the lives and minds of the main characters poses a difficult problem for the reader.

Another typical feature of modernism is the dependence on connections with earlier texts, either in the form of direct allusions or through suggestive parallels or correspondences with other works. The many Homeric correspondences are a primary example of the latter: rarely stated openly, with the obvious exceptions of the book's title and of the chapter titles that Joyce used while composing the book but chose not to include with the completed text, the connections with the *Odyssey* are nonetheless an informing presence in the novel. Although the characters are of course unaware of it, their world, as it is presented to us, often seems a transformation of Homer's. On the other hand, allusions—which range from Mulligan's quotation of Swinburne to Bloom's misquotation of *Hamlet,* and include numerous song references in Molly's monologue—tend to be more specific correspondences between the language of a passage in *Ulysses* and that of a passage or title from another work. Joyce's use of allusions and correspondences undoubtedly differs in many ways from that of Pound, Yeats, Eliot, or Woolf, but in each case, one of the reasons for calling attention to antecedent texts is to recognize the modern writer's dependence on—and at the same time, his or her appropriation of, or triumph over—various literary ancestors. It is probably no coincidence that in the early twentieth century, a time when many people felt estranged from the historical past, writers began constructing works that re-created a sense of the literary past, and presented this past as something to be controlled by modern writers for their own ends.

The modernist emphasis on literary allusions also contributed to what José Ortega y Gasset called the "dehumanization of art"—the presentation of the artistic work not as a direct representative or mirroring of life but as something shaped both by the mind and experience of an individual artist and by the conventions or discourses of the society that produced the artist.[2] Modern works often openly bear traces of their composition, as when Joyce closes *Ulysses* with the places and dates of his work on the novel: "Trieste-Zurich-Paris/ 1914–1921." The book's alternation of voices and styles, its parodic element, and even the variations in the physical appearance of the page are among the means by which *Ulysses* calls attention to its status as a literary artifact, that is, both as the product of an individual human imagination and as an assemblage of rhetorical and linguistic elements that reflect the modes of thought of a particular culture.

Joyce's shadow looms large over more recent modernist, and even postmodernist, novelists. Breon Mitchell, for instance, has documented the impact of *Ulysses* on the German novelists Henny Jahnn, Alfred Doblin, and Hermann Broch, while Vivian Mercier calls Joyce the "greatest precursor" of such *nouveau roman* writers as Michel Butor, Claude Mauriac, and Raymond Queneau.[3] As Robert Martin Adams has noted, Joyce's influence may also be detected in such novelists as Virginia Woolf, William Faulkner, Samuel Beckett, Vladimir Nabokov, Thomas Pynchon, John Barth, and Jorge Luis Borges.[4] The inwardness of modern narrative, its varied styles and perspectives, and its reliance on complex image patterns and verbal motifs may all be traced, at least in part, to *Ulysses*. Woolf's *Mrs. Dalloway*, Faulkner's *The Sound and the Fury*, Malcolm Lowry's *Under the Volcano*, and Carlos Fuentes's *A Change of Skin* are just four examples of the many novels that owe a debt to *Ulysses*. Both his vision of the modern world and his formal innovations have permanently affected the modern novel; indeed, as Norman Mailer observed in an address to the 1980 Joyce conference in Provincetown, Massachusetts, even those novelists who do not adapt Joycean narrative or stylistic strategies are affected by their knowledge of the literary possibilities opened up by Joyce's works, since they must consciously choose more traditional forms of narration rather than taking those forms for granted. While it is hard to imagine what the modern novel would be like without Joyce, it is unlikely to have developed into such a rich and subtle instrument for the interpretation of the modern world.

3 —

Critical Reception

Almost from the beginning, Joyce's books have provided critics with so much material for analysis, interpretation, and evaluation that the critical controversies they have generated often seem to overshadow the works themselves. The accumulation of critical interpretations for all of the fiction, especially *Ulysses,* undoubtedly would have pleased Joyce, who boasted that in *Ulysses* he had inserted "so many enigmas and puzzles that it will keep the professors busy for centuries" (Ellmann 521). Indeed, the entanglement of *Ulysses* with its critics began before 1922, when the book was actually published. For example, Richard Aldington's 1921 essay on "The Influence of Mr. James Joyce" (Deming 1:186–89), which opened sensibly enough with the declaration that "no valid criticism can be made of Mr. Joyce's *Ulysses* until the whole work has been published in book form," continued, nonetheless, with a fundamentally negative assessment of *Ulysses,* based on the serialized publication of about half of the total book in the *Little Review* and the *Egoist.*

Aldington associated Joyce with dadaism and naturalism, thereby faulting him on the dual grounds that the book's sylistic and technical experiments led to chaos and that its subject matter was generally low and disgusting. Similar attacks on the form and content of *Ulysses* continued through the 1920s, parried by the efforts of Joyce's defenders to make sense of the book's structure. The most famous defense during this period was T. S. Eliot's 1923 *Dial* essay, "*Ulysses*, Order and Myth" (Deming 1:268–71), an approach to *Ulysses* that functioned also as a defense of Eliot's own methods in *The Waste Land* (1922). Writing directly in response to Aldington, Eliot avoided the question whether or not *Ulysses* was, as Aldington claimed, "a tremendous libel on humanity." Instead, Eliot focused on Joyce's use of a mythical parallel as a means "of controlling, of ordering, of giving a shape and a significance to the immense panorama of futility and anarchy which is contemporary history"; this method, Eliot suggested, is "a step toward making the modern world possible for art, toward that order and form which Mr Aldington so earnestly desires." For Eliot, Joyce resembles other modernists in his discovery of a radical discontinuity that underlies our experience in the modern world, and his solution is to abandon narrative, or personal history, as the fundamental structural principle, embracing instead the coherent and universal patterns of experience found in classical myth.

Not everyone found Eliot's argument persuasive. Probably the most damaging attack came from Joyce's fellow modernist (and sometime friend) Wyndham Lewis, who devoted a chapter of his 1927 volume *Time and Western Man* to "An Analysis of the Mind of James Joyce." Lewis contended that *Ulysses* was "modern," or "progressive," only in its craftsmanship; the book's subject matter, Lewis argued, consisted largely of the residue of nineteenth-century literary naturalism as filtered through the time-obsessed philosophies of Freud, Einstein, and Bergson. Lewis regarded the novel's Homeric parallels and other structuring devices as part of an ingenious, but essentially doomed, attempt to lend the appearance of order to Joyce's "unorganized brute material . . . a suffocating, moeotic expanse of objects, all of them lifeless, the sewage of a Past twenty years old, all neatly arranged in a meticulous sequence" (Deming 1:359–60). Joyce's novel, according to Lewis, suffered from its emphasis on process, or flux, rather than on completed form; and this in turn derived from Joyce's preoccupation with the subjective inner world of aural experience rather than the more precise and objective external world of visual perception.

Joyce's response to Lewis took two forms: he satirized Lewis in *Finnegans Wake* through his depictions of the Mookse (152–59) and the Ondt (414–19), two rationalists who prefer a stable world of visual certainties to the subjective world of mystery and incertitude that Shem, the artist figure, is determined to explore; and he encouraged Stuart Gilbert to write an analysis of *Ulysses* that would address the fundamental issue raised by Lewis—the apparent contradiction between the subject matter and techniques of *Ulysses*. In *James Joyce's "Ulysses": A Study* (1930), the first significant book-length analysis of *Ulysses*, Gilbert argued that the book's techniques are, in effect, its real subject: if the characters are not fully individualized (as Lewis had charged), that is because they are primarily to be regarded in symbolic rather than realistic terms. For example, the novel's theme of recurrence, according to Gilbert, shows that the same patterns that dominated human life in Homer's time continue to appear; hence the Homeric correspondences, far from being "only an entertaining structural device or conceit," as Lewis had maintained, make an important point about the nature of human life. For Gilbert, then, the parallels with classical Greece reveal the importance of Joyce's Dubliners as modern representatives of the human condition; the Homeric analogies also demonstrate the book's fundamental coherence and the respectability of its pedigree. Through a detailed chapter-by-chapter analysis, Gilbert was also at pains to demonstrate the appropriateness of each chapter's style, narrative strategy, and images, both to the subject matter of the particular episode and to the novel as a whole.

Gilbert's book was instrumental in opening *Ulysses* to a wider audience than it had enjoyed during the 1920s, but its method of analysis seemed to many readers too schematized, too pedantic, and too often concerned with technical experimentation to account for the richness of human experience in Joyce's novel. A more satisfactory study, from this viewpoint, was *James Joyce and the Making of "Ulysses"* (1934) by Frank Budgen, an English painter who had known Joyce in Zurich during World War I. In contrast to the scholarly Gilbert, who gloried in uncovering elaborate and detailed analogies between Joyce's narrative and his source material, Budgen was straightforward and unpretentious, the sort of interpreter who did not require interpretation in turn. Budgen's study begins with an account of his first meeting with Joyce, and throughout the book he uses recollections of his conversations with Joyce as a means of revealing not only the fundamental patterns of *Ulysses* but also the man behind the work. While Gilbert had access only to the published text of *Ulysses*, Budgen had the advantage of experiencing the book first through his conversations with Joyce, as the idea for *Ulysses* formed itself in Joyce's mind. The result was a more flexible approach to the novel, one concerned less with defending the logic of the finished product than with explaining how the book evolved. Likewise, Budgen's analysis focused on technique only as a means to an end, that end being the development of Joyce's characters and their world.

Different as their interpretations of *Ulysses* were, both Gilbert and Budgen were heavily dependent on Joyce for their analyses: Budgen offered his conversations with Joyce as his primary source of information, and Gilbert consulted Joyce frequently during the composition of his study. Critics writing about *Ulysses* during the 1940s and 1950s lacked this direct access to Joyce, but they had the advantages of being able to build upon (or at times to reject) the insights of Gilbert and Budgen, and of having available the first full-length biography of Joyce, Herbert Gorman's *James Joyce* (1939). In addition, the long-awaited publication of *Finnegans Wake* (1939) contributed to an increased interest in Joyce's earlier works, and to a tendency to apply to those works the techniques of close reading and symbolic interpretation that seem appropriate to the *Wake*. Even more important for Richard M. Kain's *Fabulous Voyager: James Joyce's "Ulysses"* (1947), the one book of real significance during the period 1940–60 to be devoted entirely to *Ulysses*, were the 1937 publication of Miles L. Hanley's *Word Index to James Joyce's "Ulysses"* and Kain's discovery that Joyce relied extensively on *Thom's Dublin Directory* for 1904—a later edition of a book found on Leopold Bloom's shelves (17.1362/708)—as a source of information about the city and its inhabitants.

Both the concordance and the postal directory helped Kain to see significant connections between one part of *Ulysses* and another. Abandoning the chapter-by-chapter method of analysis favored by Gilbert and Budgen, Kain viewed *Ulysses* from a broader angle, tracing a variety of themes and stylistic and structural elements throughout the book. Four appendices, listing aspects of Bloom's life and character, references to other characters in the book, references to specific Dublin shops and buildings, and occurrences of verbal motifs, help to emphasize the "tonal and structural unity"[1] of the book that Kain set out to demonstrate.

Analyses of Joyce's work in general that contributed significantly to the increasing interest in *Ulysses* during the 1940s and 1950s include those by Harry Levin (*James Joyce: A Critical Introduction*, 1941), William York Tindall (*James Joyce: His Way of Interpreting the Modern World*, 1950; *A Reader's Guide to James Joyce*, 1959), and Hugh Kenner (*Dublin's Joyce*, 1956). Fundamentally different in their approaches to Joyce, these three scholars exhibit the range of methodologies that have dominated American criticism of *Ulysses*. Levin's perspective on Joyce was that of a comparatist: like Edmund Wilson, whose *Axel's Castle* (1931) contained an influential chapter on Joyce, Levin placed Joyce squarely within the mainstream of the European literary tradition. Along with Kain, Levin was one of the critics most responsible for redirecting *Ulysses* criticism toward the book's human values and away from the pyrotechnics of symbolism, narrative strategies, and stylistic innovation. Tindall, on the other hand, was a freewheeling deep reader whose ad hoc symbolic interpretations often combined brilliant insights with undiscriminating, and sometimes conflicting, claims that overlooked the obvious in search of the arcane. His studies were enormously popular with students, however, and they opened up legitimate avenues of inquiry that have been followed by other scholars.

Kenner's work has had a more lasting influence on Joyce studies than that of Levin or Tindall, in part because Kenner has continued to write on Joyce and to develop new and intriguing approaches to the work. Declaring that "Joyce's Dublin was in fact an eighteenth-century parody,"[2] Kenner read *Ulysses* as a modernist variation on neoclassical satire, and stressed the ironic elements in Joyce's language, characterization, and narrative strategies. Rather than dispute Wyndham Lewis's argument that Joyce's characters were stereotypical, Kenner argued that they were "walking clichés, because the [real] Dubliners were." For Kenner, Joyce was basically an ironist who critiqued his society by reproducing, and thereby calling attention to, its language: "Joyce was hardly more word-conscious than his characters were. So the usual criterion of style, that it disappear like glass before the reality of the subject, doesn't apply to his pages. The language of Dublin *is* the subject; his books are about words, the complexity is there, in the way people talk, and Joyce copes with it by making it impossible for us to ignore the word on the page."[3] Kenner has expanded upon, and refined, his approach in more recent books on Joyce (*Joyce's Voices*, 1978; "*Ulysses*," 1980) as well as in studies that view Joyce within a broader context (notably, *Flaubert, Joyce and Beckett: The Stoic Comedians*, 1962; *The Pound Era*, 1971; and *A Colder Eye: The Modern Irish Writers*, 1983). Even many critics who disagree with his fundamentally ironic readings of *Ulysses*, and the fiction generally, have been influenced by his demonstration that the form and content of the books are inseparable.

If Kenner refocused attention on Joyce's language, the publication of Richard Ellmann's monumental *James Joyce* (1959; revised, 1982) opened up Joyce's life as a key to the interpretation of his works. Far more thorough and objective in its presentation than Gorman's biography, which was written under Joyce's direction, Ellmann's book provided critics and general readers not only with an extended factual history of Joyce's life and continual insights into the many facets of his mind, but also with numerous connections between the life and the work. Ellmann's was a genuinely critical biography, and if it had its weaknesses—as when Ellmann relied on the early fiction as a source of information about Joyce's life or pushed too hard for connections between biographical and fictional events—it nonetheless served an important function in calling attention to the reality, and fallibility, of the man behind the books.

Joyce's fallibility, and his reliance on materials that can be tested for their reality (newspaper stories, for example), led Robert Martin Adams to undertake the investigations that culminated in his *Surface and Symbol: The Consistency of James Joyce's "Ulysses"* (1962). Adams debunked both the idea that Joyce was incapable of error and the belief that every element in the text was susceptible to symbolic interpretation. In so doing, he served an important function, helping to separate the grain of solid critical analysis from the chaff of wildly speculative readings. (More recently, a similar role has been played by Paul van Caspel's *Bloomers on the Liffey: Eisegetical Readings of Joyce's "Ulysses"* [1986], which is primarily a discussion of misreadings of *Ulysses*, many of them by prominent critics.) In addition, Adams uncovered sources for many of the events, phrases, and characters in *Ulysses*, and thereby provided important material for such later reference volumes as Weldon Thornton's *Allusions in "Ulysses"* (1968) and Don Gifford and Robert J. Seidman's *Notes for Joyce: An Annotation of James Joyce's "Ulysses"* (1974). Along with A. Walton Litz's *The Art of James Joyce: Method and Design in "Ulysses" and "Finnegans Wake"* (1961), Adams's book also helped to lay the groundwork for subsequent studies of Joyce's composition process, by emphasizing the fact that *Ulysses* was not conceived whole and written down in final form but evolved in Joyce's mind from the materials he had at hand.

In its insistence on the importance of understanding the literal world on which Joyce drew, and its resistance to symbolic readings except when they can be shown to be "consistent" with the realistic surface of *Ulysses*, Adams aligned himself with a growing minority of critics who rejected the symbol-hunting tendencies of much of the "Joyce Industry." Two others whose work helped to correct exigetical excesses were S. L. Goldberg (*The Classical Temper: A Study of James Joyce's "Ulysses,"* 1961) and Stanley Sultan (*The Argument of "Ulysses,"* 1964). Whereas Stuart Gilbert had called attention to the book's mythic correspondences, symbolic patterns, and narrative styles, Goldberg and Sultan focused on its human element—its development of human situations and the implication of its presentation of its characters' lives. Both Goldberg and Sultan clearly believed that Joyce's strength lay in his powers as a realistic novelist: Goldberg, for instance, was skeptical of the artistic value of Joyce's stylistic experimentation in the later chapters of *Ulysses*, while Sultan argued that symbolic interpretations must be grounded in, and directly related to, the book's realistic action. Sultan has reiterated his position recently, in an essay that argues for the primacy of fictional events in *Ulysses* over the techniques used in the narration of those events.[4]

Despite Sultan's turn from technique to story, many of the most interesting and influential critical studies of the past two decades have focused on Joyce's stylistic and narrational modes. In one way or another, David Hayman's *"Ulysses": The Mechanics of Meaning* (1970; revised, 1982), Marilyn French's *The Book as World: James Joyce's "Ulysses"* (1976), Hugh Kenner's *Joyce's Voices* (1978) and *"Ulysses"* (1980; revised, 1986), Karen Lawrence's *The Odyssey of Style in "Ulysses"* (1981), Brook Thomas's *James Joyce's "Ulysses": A Book of Many Happy Returns* (1982), and Fritz Senn's *Joyce's Dislocutions: Essays on Reading as Translation* (1984) have all dealt with questions of language, structure, narrative perspective, "reflexivity," and the like, rather than with symbolism, characterization, and the other questions addressed by more traditional critics. Among the most influential developments within this time have been Hayman's suggestion that the variations in narrative style may be attributed to the presence of an "arranger" and Kenner's development of the "Uncle Charles Principle" as an explanation of the way in which descriptions of characters seem to be couched in terminology especially appropriate to those particular persons. Nonetheless, other approaches remain an important part of *Ulysses* criticism: Michael Groden examines Joyce's composition process in *"Ulysses" in Progress* (1977); Michael Seidel deals with the Homeric theme in *Epic Geography: James Joyce's "Ulysses"* (1976); Cheryl Herr, in *Joyce's Anatomy of Culture* (1986), demonstrates the extent to which Joyce developed his materials out of the "institutional discourses" that prevailed in late-nineteenth- and early-twentieth-century Dublin; and in *Joyce's Uncertainty Principle* (1987),

Phillip F. Herring shows that *Ulysses* shares with Joyce's other works an incessant concern with linguistic, structural, and thematic mysteries that often cannot be resolved with utter certainty.

The consensus of critical opinion is that *Ulysses* occupies a central position in the history of the modern novel, a position analogous to the one occupied by *The Waste Land* within poetry of the modernist age. Joyce is now annually subjected to more published studies than any other modern author (Faulkner places a strong second); in recent years annual Joyce symposia, alternating between meetings in North America and Europe, have provided scholars with additional opportunities to display their critical wares. Even discarding those studies that are wrongheaded, unoriginal, or impenetrable, there is still a remarkable amount of useful material devoted each year to Joyce's works, which remain firmly entrenched within the canon of modern literature; and within the field of Joyce scholarship, *Ulysses* is the work most frequently studied, analyzed, cited, and used as a text for expounding upon new critical theories. The dual attractiveness of Joyce's novel seems to reside both in its superb artistry and in the humanity of its situation and characters. In the following analyses, I shall emphasize both the book's techniques and its rich account of human experience, two inseparable aspects of *Ulysses* that have attracted readers for nearly seven decades.

A READING

Arrangements of Reality

Despite its reputation for narrative difficulty, *Ulysses* opens with a generally straightforward example of third-person narration:

> Stately, plump Buck Mulligan came from the stairhead, bearing a bowl of lather on which a mirror and a razor lay crossed. A yellow dressinggown, ungirdled, was sustained gently behind him on the mild morning air. He held the bowl aloft and intoned:
> —*Introibo ad altare Dei.* (1.1–5 / 3)

Later, the reader might wonder whether to construe "Stately" as an adjective or as an adverb, and so might discover a problem where at first none seemed to exist. (This, by the way, is a common occurrence in reading *Ulysses:* something that once seemed perfectly clear turns out, on closer inspection, to be ambiguous.) A first reading, however, is apt to pose no problems until we reach the Latin, and even there the possible hindrances to understanding—the absence of quotation marks and the recitation of a passage from the Latin mass—are unlikely to be much of an obstacle for alert readers. Within a few chapters, however, the style will change drastically, and new elements or perspectives will be introduced each time we become comfortable with a given viewpoint.

An example is the following passage, taken from the description of the funeral procession in Hades. When Bloom advocates transporting corpses by "municipal funeral trams like they have in Milan," Martin Cunningham supports Bloom's idea:

> —And, Martin Cunningham said, we wouldn't have scenes like that when the hearse capsized round Dunphy's and upset the coffin on to the road.
> —That was terrible, Mr Power's shocked face said, and the corpse fell about the road. Terrible!
> —First round Dunphy's, Mr Dedalus said, nodding. Gordon Bennett cup.
> —Praises be to God! Martin Cunningham said piously.
> Bom! Upset. A coffin bumped out on to the road. Burst open. Paddy Dignam shot out and rolling over stiff in the dust in a brown habit too large for him. Red face: grey now. Mouth fallen open. Asking what's up now. (6.415–23/98)

The natural inclination will be to read "Bom! Upset," and the rest, as the narrator's description of an event occurring before our eyes: just as the characters discuss an earlier incident in which a hearse overturned, the same thing happens again, this time to the hearse carrying Paddy Dignam's corpse. When the procession continues undisturbed by this event, however, and Bloom thinks, "But suppose now it did happen. Would he bleed if a nail say cut him in the knocking about?" we know that we have read something other than a description of a current event, so we may turn to the alternate hypothesis that the entire paragraph is an example of interior monologue, or direct presentation of a character's thoughts without an intervening narrator. That's closer to the mark; but while "Red face: grey now. Mouth fallen open. Asking what's up now," and so forth, resembles the style of Bloom's thoughts as we see them elsewhere, the description of the coffin falling open is more like a sketch of a nonverbal scene that flashes through Bloom's mind, a description followed immediately by a commentary.

Arrangements of Reality

One of the points here is that as *Ulysses* proceeds, its language increasingly finds uses other than those found in most novels. David Hayman has accounted for some of the more experimental aspects of the later chapters by positing the existence of an "arranger," a form of narrator who is more concerned with playing linguistic games than with telling a story.[1] This explanation is useful as long as we realize that all of the narrative styles and forms in *Ulysses* are variations on Joyce's basic role as the artificer who creates, sustains, and at times manipulates his fictional world.[2] Like Eliot, who acted as a sort of ventriloquist in *The Waste Land* (a role suggested by Eliot's original title for the poem, "He Do the Police in Different Voices"), Joyce adopts numerous narrative disguises or poses, structuring reality first one way and then another, as he examines his world from several distinct angles.

Ulysses proclaims at every turn its author's control over the fictional world that it depicts, and his refusal to allow any single perspective to dominate our judgments. Thus, an event that is seen or remembered from one viewpoint will later be viewed from the perspective of another character; one style will compete with another, not only between chapters but also within them (as in Aeolus, where the headings introduce ironic perspectives on the narration and dialogue, or in Oxen of the Sun, which runs the gamut of English prose styles); allusions to and correspondences with other literary works suggest alternative interpretations of a given statement or event; the impression of realism jostles against surreal effects and stylistic parodies; and, while setting up the illusion of objective reality, Joyce introduces into his text inconsistencies, errors, ambiguity, and other signs of narrative unreliability. By such means, Joyce forces the reader into an active role in the novel. In the end, Joyce's aim includes making us re-examine all of the assumptions that we brought with us on our first (and perhaps our twenty-first) reading of *Ulysses*.

Joyce's materials were so vast and broad-ranging that he needed a controlling device to hold them in suspension. He fastened on the *Odyssey*, and there is evidence that he tried to develop, or at least allowed, numerous correspondences between the Homeric epic and his own book. Eventually, however, he feared that he might have oversystema-tized *Ulysses*. Joyce's aversion to rigid schemata is evident throughout the novel, and it is one of the lessons most necessary for readers to learn: like Odysseus, we need to be men and women of many ways, always ready to consider matters from a new perspective. The Cyclopean view-point of the Citizen—an Irish patriot who makes no secret of his dislike of foreigners—in the twelfth chapter is an extreme example of single-mindedness: he is easy to parody because he has no depth, no access to alternative views. As an illustration of a broader vision we might cite Leopold Bloom's attempt to see himself from a cat's angle of percep-tion: "Wonder what I look like to her. Height of a tower? No, she can jump me" (4.28–29/55). Bloom's willingness to see himself from an external viewpoint and to entertain and discard a hypothesis stands in sharp contrast to the more limited minds of most of the other characters in *Ulysses*. If we were seeking a model of openmindedness, we would search Joyce's pages in vain for a better example than Bloom.

Bloom's interest in parallax suggests one way in which we could view the book's various styles and perspectives. Parallax involves the juxtaposition of two distinct viewpoints, as when an astronomer views a heavenly body from two different locations. Each of the book's styles may be regarded as a sighting of an object, and it is only by comparing different sightings that we can gain anything like the true perspective that we seek. In Cyclops, for example, there is a constant alternation between two styles, one of which inflates whatever it describes while the other diminishes every object of its attention. Neither viewpoint represents the truth, nor do two wrong perspectives make a right one, but by exposing the distorted or inadequate values implied by two kinds of language, Joyce hints at another set of values that perhaps cannot be expressed directly but are embodied by the totality of *Ulys-ses* and, particularly, by the characterization of Bloom.[3]

Joyce introduces the concept of parallax in the Lestrygonians chapter, where Bloom directs his attention to ethereal matters in an attempt to avoid thinking about his wife's impending affair with Blazes Boylan:

> Mr Bloom moved forward, raising his troubled eyes. Think no
> more about that. After one. Timeball on the ballastoffice is down.
> Dunsink time. Fascinating little book that is of sir Robert Ball's.
> Parallax. I never exactly understood. There's a priest. Could ask
> him. Par it's Greek: parallel, parallax. Met him pike hoses she called
> it till I told her about the transmigration. O rocks! (8.108–13/154)

This passage provides us with a good example of the associative logic
underlying Bloom's stream of consciousness. The name of Robert Ball
emerges from Bloom's thoughts of a timeball (reinforced visually, for
the reader, by "*ball*astoffice"), and a difference in time zones—for
example, why Dunsink time, by which much Dublin business was
conducted, is twenty-five minutes earlier than Greenwich time—can
be explained by referring to parallax. Equally intriguing is the process
through which Bloom's thoughts circulate back to an aspect of the
subject he has been avoiding: Molly. "After one" seems initially to be
merely a comment on the time of day, but in fact the countdown to
Boylan's expected 4:00 P.M. arrival at Bloom's house has begun. Likewise, one "Greek" word (parallax) suggests another (metempsychosis), and that in turn leads to Bloom's thoughts both of Molly's mispronunciation, omitted in the original scene but supplied here, and of
Molly's exclamation of impatience at Bloom's definition of metempsychosis: "O, rocks! she said. Tell us in plain words" (4.343/64). Moreover, since Molly's "rocks" are the equivalent of "balls," the passage
has recylced back to its origins both in Molly's sexual adventure and in
the ball imagery of the timeball/ ballastoffice/ Robert Ball triad.

   While Bloom's thoughts reveal both his association of similar
ideas and his obsessive concern with Molly, however, they also reveal
relationships that go well beyond what Bloom consciously or unconsciously knows—relationships that are fundamental to the narrative
and thematic logic of *Ulysses*. It is true that the terms *parallax* and
metempsychosis are both derived from the Greek, but it is perhaps
more important that their relationship to one another, as thematic
components in *Ulysses,* is dependent upon our recognizing that the
Homeric correspondences in the book are simultaneously examples of

metempsychosis (since Odysseus is figuratively reborn in Bloom) and parallax (since the parallels with the Greek world serve to suggest an alternative viewpoint or perspective on the modern world). While parts of *Ulysses* appear at first to be little more than the presentation of what Wyndham Lewis called "unorganized brute material" (Deming 1:359), an encounter with virtually any passage will reveal an intricate ordering of relationships both within the passage and in its recapitulation of elements found elsewhere in the book. That the significance of these passages exists primarily for the readers rather than for the characters is reasonable, since as Marilyn French has noted, "the novel happens to us, not to them."[4] Likewise, it is a mistake to assume that *Ulysses* is simply a transcription of a series of fictional events whose significance is limited to what the characters know, or could know, about their lives and their world: what we see in *Ulysses* is not merely a transcribed reality but an arranged one, and its significance lies in that arrangement just as much as it does in the materials that Joyce puts in order.

In Sirens, for example, the narration constantly undermines our assumption that there is a natural order to reality, giving us instead a series of interpolations that depend for their effect on our recognizing the intrusion of elements from earlier chapters of *Ulysses*. Like *Tristram Shandy,* in which Eugenius reads an earlier volume of the novel in which he appears (and contends with Tristram about the meaning of a word in that book),[5] Sirens is a highly self-conscious narration in which the narrator alludes directly to earlier episodes. Hence, Bloom's dietary habits, introduced at the beginning of Calypso in punning fashion—"Mr Leopold Bloom ate with relish the inner organs of beasts and fowls" (4.1–2/55)—are recalled in Sirens: "As said before he ate with relish the inner organs . . ." and "Bloom ate liv as said before" (11.519–20/269, 11.569/271). While it is common enough for narrators to reveal their awareness that their words exist in a book, however, it is far more unusual to see characters who appear somehow aware of the terms in which their lives are narrated. Yet there are at least two events in Sirens that cannot be explained by a cause-and-effect logic that is limited to the actions in which the characters are involved. Instead, these events suggest that the narration is influencing the events of the chapter.

The first of these events occurs as Blazes Boylan is leaving the bar on his way to an assignation with Molly:

> —I'm off, said Boylan with impatience.
> He slid his chalice brisk away, grasped his change.
> —Wait a shake, begged Lenehan, drinking quickly. I wanted to tell you. Tom Rochford . . .
> —Come on to blazes, said Blazes Boylan, going.
> Lenehan gulped to go.
> —Got the horn or what? he said. Wait. I'm coming. (11.426–32/ 267)

Here, Lenehan's sudden recollection that he is supposed to talk with Boylan about Tom Rochford's invention is apparently triggered by the narrator's phrase, "said Boylan with impatience," which echoes the joke Tom Rochford made earlier: when Lenehan said he would sound Boylan out about the invention, Rochford replied, "Tell him I'm Boylan with impatience" (10.486/232). That the observation of a physical event influences the event itself is a principle first articulated by Werner Heisenberg in 1930, eight years after the publication of *Ulysses*, yet here we have a passage that suggests a corollary to Heisenberg's principle of indeterminacy: not only may the narration of a fictional event influence the reader's interpretation of the event, it may also help to create the event. In this case, unless we want to assume that the juxtaposition of the narrator's pun and Lenehan's remembrance is coincidental, we are forced to conclude that Lenehan has been influenced by the narration of the book in which he is a character.

The second example occurs only two pages later, as Ben Dollard recalls Molly Bloom's business in secondhand ("left off") clothing:

> —By God, she had some luxurious operacloaks and things there.
> Mr Dedalus wandered back, pipe in hand.
> —Merrion square style. Balldresses, by God, and court dresses. He

31

wouldn't take any money either. What? Any God's quantity of cocked hats and boleros and trunkhose. What?

—Ay, ay, Mr Dedalus nodded. Mrs Marion Bloom has left off clothes of all descriptions.

Jingle jaunted down the quays. Blazes sprawled on bounding tyres.

Liver and bacon. Steak and kidney pie. Right, sir. Right, Pat. Mrs Marion. Met him pike hoses. Smell of burn. Of Paul de Kock. Nice name he. (11.491–501/269)

The last paragraph refers to Bloom's conversation with Molly in Calypso. "Met him pike hoses" was Molly's mispronunciation of "metempsychosis" (although this information is withheld from the reader until the Lestrygonians chapter, where Bloom recalls, "Met him pike hoses she called it till I told her about the transmigration" [8.112–13/154]); the burning smell emanated from the kidney that Bloom left to fry while he went upstairs; and the passage concludes with an echo of Molly's request for a new book—"Get another of Paul de Kock's. Nice name he has" (4.358/64). As for "Mrs Marion," that appellation originated, within the pages of Ulysses, in the letter addressed in Boylan's "Bold hand" to "Mrs Marion Bloom" (4.244/61). The fact that the letter was addressed to Molly in her own name (rather than to Mrs. Leopold Bloom) is for Bloom an omen of her adulterous affair with Boylan, since it suggests that Boylan regards her as an independent woman, not as Bloom's wife.

In the passage above, it might seem at first that Bloom's train of thought is initiated by Simon's recollection of the advertisement for secondhand clothing, which coincidentally referred to Molly as "Mrs Marion Bloom." In fact, however, Bloom and Simon are in different rooms, far enough apart so that Bloom cannot hear the conversation that appears to stimulate his interior monologue. In view of Bloom's role as a double for the reader of Ulysses—the subject of the last chapter of this study—it seems logical to regard Bloom's thoughts as having been prompted by his reading of the text in which he exists, or at least by a momentary merging of Bloom with the reader. The passage does more than reveal Joyce's technical virtuosity, however, since it implies a connection between Molly's situation now, when she is about to declare some measure of independence from her husband by having an affair, and during the time when Bloom was out of a job and Molly was forced to support the family. The sly pun in "left off clothes of all descriptions"—a phrase uttered not too long before Molly will take off her clothes for Boylan—reinforces the parallel between the two times when Molly's independence will be revealed through the designation "Mrs Marion Bloom."[6]

As the examples above indicate, *Ulysses* continually tests the line of demarcation between traditional novelistic design and postmodernist confrontations with language as a closed system. *Ulysses* sets forth, side by side, elements of realism and antirealism; it proclaims itself both a world and a book. That the narration of events may sometimes assume a more prominent role than the events themselves becomes clear when, for example, successive sentences or paragraphs narrate much the same information in two different ways (7.21–24 / 116, 11.778–88 / 276–77). In calling attention to the narration, the book requires that we consider the origins, and hence the status, validity, and authority, of the words on the page. Hugh Kenner has astutely noted that when the narrator of the *Dubliners* story "Eveline" indirectly quotes Eveline's suitor, Frank, to the effect that "He had fallen on his feet in Buenos Ayres," we might suppose that Frank's phrasing derives from the sort of cheap romantic fiction that would be likely to appeal to Eveline.[7] More recently, Kenner, Fritz Senn, Paul van Caspel, and Heather Cook Callow have all argued that when Stephen thinks that the tower key "is mine. I paid the rent" (1.631 / 20), he is actually quoting Mulligan's words rather than claiming to have paid the rent himself.[8] The possibility that Stephen might be the transmitter, rather than the source, of these words obviously affects our interpretation of the passage, but it also has a peculiar revelance to Joyce's work, in which the artist is continually presented to us not as the originator of language but as an appropriator and reshaper of a language that precedes and, in a sense, creates him.

A similar concern with the origins of language may be detected in the Sirens passage cited earlier, where we might speculate on the source of Simon Dedalus's quip, "Mrs Marion Bloom has left off clothes of all descriptions." The initial assumption might be that Simon, whose wit is amply displayed in *A Portrait* as well as *Ulysses*, is solely responsible for the witticism, but it is equally likely that he is recalling the actual advertisement that Molly ran for her dealings in secondhand clothing. If so, the passage is doubly ironic in the way it serves as a bridge to Bloom's preoccupation with the assignation between Molly and Boylan, for whatever advertisement Molly put in the paper would undoubtedly have been written by Bloom himself.

Ulysses concerns itself in other ways with the origins of words. For example, the extensive use of literary allusions, in dialogue or otherwise, involves the reader of *Ulysses* with antecedent texts wherein the borrowed words appear. The "headlines" of Aeolus, which Joyce added at a late stage in the composition of *Ulysses*, are another instance of words whose origins pose a problem for the reader. Karen Lawrence has noted that these headings, which are visually distinct from the chapter's narrative, "represent a discourse generated in the text that advertises the fact that it is 'written,' anonymous, and public—that is, cut off from any single originating consciousness." Moreover, she maintains, the headings "represent anonymous, collective discourse," stemming as they do from the popular press.[9] The headings challenge our notion of a unitary consciousness behind the novel not only because they are parodies of an impersonal, collective discourse, but also because their presence on the page cannot be attributed to the chapter's dominant narrative voice; and these distinct Aeolian styles differ, in turn, from (say) the playful narrative voice of Scylla and Charybdis, which engages in wordplay at the expense of the characters assembled in the library, or from the arranging presence of Wandering Rocks, where a series of distinct narratives intrude upon one another, disturbing our sense of narrative cohesion.

In each case, there is evidence that language, in *Ulysses*, does not merely represent an existing reality but shapes, and even transforms, it, as for example when the Lestrygonians narrator's description of Cashel Boyle O'Connor Fitzmaurice Tisdall Farrell's hat—"Tight as a skullpiece a tiny hat gripped his head"—becomes more literal: "Mr

Bloom walked on again easily, seeing ahead of him in sunlight the tight skullpiece" (8.296–97, 8.315–16 / 159). Not only do these passages call into question the relationship between Bloom's perspective and the narrator's descriptions, but they demonstrate the ease with which figurative description may attain the status of apparent objectivity. On a broader scale, and in more complex fashion, the same problem pervades Oxen of the Sun, Circe, Eumaeus, and Ithaca, for in each episode the origins, authority, and status of the chapter's language are among its central concerns.

Marilyn French has contended that "hovering behind all Joyce's work is the notion that language and reality are one." Early attempts in Joyce's fiction to distinguish sincere and insincere language from one another give way, French argues, to the recognition that reality is "an unknowable ultimate," so that in *Ulysses*, "Even the worst jargon, the tritest phrase, scientific, journalistic, and military language express some sliver of truth about human experience."[10] If language cannot be directly expressive of reality, at least it can give us one version of the truth, allowing us to see first through one glass, and then through another, but always darkly. Human language, imperfect instrument that it is, naturally tends toward error; yet error, for Joyce, is one of the means by which we arrive at some understanding or approximation of the truth. The many styles and perspectives of *Ulysses* are related, in this sense, to the factual errors and rumors that proliferate throughout the novel: they expose, for the reader, a particular vision or logic that bears a skewed relationship to the larger truth expressed, indirectly, by the novel. Moving from questions of linguistic to those of factual accuracy, then, in the next two chapters I will explore related aspects of this larger problem, showing that error and rumor play a significant role in shaping the form and vision of *Ulysses*.

5 ——

A Comedy of Errors

Unlike Odysseus, who knows that his bed cannot be moved because he constructed it out of a rooted olive tree, Leopold Bloom knows that his own bed was purchased by Molly's father at the governor's auction in Gibraltar and transported to Dublin (4.60–62/56, 15.3289/547). Unfortunately, what Bloom "knows" turns out not to be true: we learn from Molly that the bed was bought from "old Cohen" rather than Lord Napier (18.1212–14/772), and the improbability that anyone would move such a bed from Gibraltar to Dublin suggests that it was more likely to have been purchased in Dublin. If this is so, we have a contrast not only between Homer's rooted bed and Joyce's movable one, but also between the long journey taken by the bed in Bloom's imagination and the brief journey it took in "reality." Bloom is equally mistaken in accepting Molly's interpretations of the initials I.H.S. and I.N.R.I. in Catholic ritual; in his own ad hoc translation of Italian *teco* ("with you") as "tonight"; and in his belief that Herrick's "Bid me to live, and I will live/ Thy protestant to be" is a religious poem rather than a love lyric (5.372–74/81, 8.1051–52/180, 16.1742–43/661). When Stephen is knocked down by a British soldier and half-consciously mumbles fragments from Yeats's poem "Who Goes with Fergus?" Bloom hears a reference to a more palpable reality: "Ferguson, I think I caught. A girl. Some girl. Best thing could happen him" (15.4950–51/609). Later, in the cabman's shelter, Bloom persists in this mistake, even speculating silently that "Miss Ferguson . . . was very possibly the particular lodestar who brought him down to Irishtown so early in the morning" (16.1559–61/656). These misunderstandings are typical of Bloom's encounter with Stephen and, indeed, of Bloom's world, which is generally a composite of facts and errors, shrewd insights jostling against misconceptions. Few characters in literature make more errors of fact or interpretation than Bloom, whose day might almost be reduced to a series of missed encounters with the truth.

Toward the end of the fourth chapter of *A Portrait of the Artist as a Young Man,* however, Stephen connects both life and art with error: "To live, to err, to fall, to triumph, to recreate life out of life!" (172). To err is, figuratively, to wander (Latin *errare*), and what Stephen seems to be proposing for himself is a circular path in which a wandering from the truth leads back toward it. The path of indirection or wandering is a familiar one in Joyce's fiction, as when Stephen proposes that "the shortest way to Tara was *via* Holyhead" (*Portrait* 250), a statement that makes sense in Stephen's mental geography if not on maps of the British Isles. In *Ulysses,* where the bulk of the action is given over to the wanderings of the modern-day Odysseus, who is also (ironically) compared to the Wandering Jew (as Stephen is to Yeats's Wandering Aengus), virtually everything wanders: the book has no fixed viewpoint or narrative style, and in later chapters its dialogue is less a representation of what characters actually say than a version of their words colored by the style of the surrounding narration; the tenth chapter presents the Dublin citizenry as a collection of wandering rocks; Bloom's thoughts constantly wander; and Molly strays from marital fidelity to enjoy the excitement of an affair. As errancy is a major aspect of the technique and narrative pattern of *Ulysses,* it is also one of the book's richest and most intriguing themes, one related to Joyce's characterization, to his treatment of authority, and to the reader's active involvement in the text.

Phillip F. Herring has shown that Joyce's use of error to call attention to his characters' "ignorance or vulgarity" is a significant aspect of the fiction as early as *Dubliners*.[1] Equally revealing but far more numerous are the errors made by characters in *Ulysses*. In the second chapter, for instance, Stephen conducts a history lesson for his class and then collects his salary from Mr. Deasy, who lectures Stephen on fiscal prudence, the evils of Jews and women, and the lessons of Irish history. The authority of his views on the other subjects is weak enough anyway, but it is further diminished by the inaccuracy of his account of history, for as Adams has demonstrated, "all his notions of history are upside down."[2] Contrary to what Mr. Deasy says, the Orange lodges did not oppose the union of Great Britain and Ireland "twenty years before O'Connell did," nor did his own ancestor Sir John Blackwood vote for the Act of Union (2.270–83 / 31); Devorgilla, the "faithless wife" whom he credits with having brought the English into Ireland (2.392–94 / 34–35), was married to O'Rourke but ran off with MacMurrough (Deasy gets the men in her life reversed); and there is no evidence that the aphorism that the sun never sets on the British Empire may be traced to a "French Celt" (2.248–49 / 30). Deasy is equally mistaken in his assessment of Stephen as a Fenian (an ardent Irish nationalist), and in his reference to "the prelates of [Stephen's] communion," which implies that Stephen is a practicing Catholic (2.271–72 / 31). His parting shot—the lame joke that Ireland "never persecuted the jews" because "she never let them in" (2.438–42 / 36)—is wrong on both counts: small numbers of Jews had been living in Ireland for centuries, with the population increasing significantly in the nineteenth century, and while anti-Semitism was a less prominent factor in Ireland than elsewhere in Europe, there was a serious and well-publicized outbreak of anti-Semitism in Limerick beginning early in 1904, only months before the action of *Ulysses*.[3]

In Scylla and Charybdis, Stephen declares that "A man of genius makes no mistakes. His errors are volitional and are the portals of discovery" (9.228–29 / 190). Mr. Deasy is hardly a genius, and his errors are certainly not volitional, but they do serve as portals of discovery for readers who recognize the gap between Mr. Deasy's version of history and more conventional renditions. Likewise, Bloom's errors allow us to see the way his mind works, and to judge the range and depth of his imagination. Occasionally Bloom corrects his own mistakes, as when he first remembers a line from Mozart's *Don Giovanni* as *Voglio e non vorrei* and later remembers it, correctly, as *Vorrei e non vorrei* (4.327/64, 6.238/93) or when he thinks that the Ballast Office timeball falls at one o'clock Dunsink time, which he subsequently corrects to one o'clock Greenwich time (8.109/154, 8.571/167). Not only are the errors themselves devices by which Joyce calls attention to major themes—the seduction motif of the *Don Giovanni* duet, the parallax theme of Greenwich and Dunsink time zones—but the pattern in which Bloom's mind recircles back to a subject and corrects an earlier error suggests the experience of the reader whose own errors and misjudgments are subject to correction on a subsequent encounter with the text.

Not that Bloom typically recognizes his own mistakes, or that his emendations are always improvements. Bloom's judgment that Mercadante's *Seven Last Words of Christ* is "splendid" (5.403–4/82) demonstrates the inadequacy of his taste in music since, as Zack Bowen has noted, this Lenten oratorio is generally favored by "the uninitiated"; his later misattribution of the work to Meyerbeer (11.1275/290, 16.1737–38/661) indicates that his factual knowledge of music is as unreliable as his taste.[4] On most subjects, Bloom's knowledge is generally eclectic and superficial: typically, he knows enough about a subject to make mistakes that a more ignorant person would never make. While noting his many errors, then—his misquotation of *Hamlet,* for example (8.67–68/152), or his curious belief that a nun invented barbed wire (8.154/155, 13.811–13/369)—we should remember that Bloom's mistakes are the result of a lively mind, and that his willingness to admit error is a more admirable trait than the parochialism, obstinacy, and lack of self-awareness demonstrated by some of the other characters in *Ulysses.*

Errors of a different sort are those that cannot be attributed directly to Bloom, or to any other character in the book, but emerge from the narration. The problem is especially prevalent in Ithaca, whose catechistic form and recitation of "facts" serves as part of the narrative pose of objective reliability, while a host of errors and inconsistencies suggest an altogether different perspective on the subject. Since a large percentage of the factual material that we are given in *Ulysses*—dates, ages, family history, Bloom's weight, the contents of Bloom's drawer and the books on his shelves—comes from Ithaca, it is important to note that the chapter probably contains more erroneous or skewed information than any other one in the book. Even in declaring what seems at first a simple fact—that "there remained a period of 10 years, 5 months and 18 days" since the Blooms last had intercourse (17.2282–84 / 736)—the narrator errs by counting from the birth of their son, Rudy, rather than from "5 weeks previous, viz. 27 November 1893," when complete intercourse between Bloom and Molly ceased. The unreliability of the Ithacan catechist is one means by which we might observe the inadequacy of a purely empirical viewpoint to account for the reality of human experience.

Errors of fact continue through *Ulysses,* relatively late examples being Molly's subtraction of a year from her age (18.475 / 751) and her exaggeration of Bloom's late arrival home (at 18.927 / 764 she is irritated at Bloom's "coming in at 4 in the morning," but the next church bell, at 18.1231–32 / 772, reveals that it is now only 2:45). More closely related to the reader's encounter with the text are the many instances of misunderstanding or misinterpretation on the part of the characters, some of which are cleared up while others go uncorrected. In the Nausicaa chapter, Gerty MacDowell's romantic and sentimental view of Bloom ("He was in deep mourning, she could see that, and the story of a haunting sorrow was written on his face" [13.421–22 / 357]) stands corrected for the reader, who experiences a sharp shift to Bloom's perspective, while Gerty remains unaware that her image of Bloom is essentially an extension of her own perspective. For that matter, the Cyclops narrator's reference to Bloom as a cadger—"Bloom putting in his old goo with his twopenny stump that he cadged off of Joe" (12.682–83 / 310–11)—surely fits his own character better than Bloom's. Both passages serve as warnings of the extent to which projections of ourselves may color our interpretations of fictional or real events.

A Comedy of Errors

Misunderstanding is a frequent theme in *Ulysses*, an early example being the milkwoman's belief that Haines is speaking to her in French, when in fact he is speaking Irish. Haines himself will go astray as he tries to follow Mulligan's explanation of Stephen's *Hamlet* theory:

> —Pooh! Buck Mulligan said. We have grown out of Wilde and paradoxes. It's quite simple. He proves by algebra that Hamlet's grandson is Shakespeare's grandfather and that he himself is the ghost of his own father.
> —What? Haines said, beginning to point at Stephen. He himself?
> (1.554–58 / 18)

Haines's mistake is understandable, since Mulligan's summary is garbled, but it is also significant that Haines misinterprets "he himself" as a reference to Stephen, since this points to the connection between Stephen's life and his reading of *Hamlet*. The confusion of pronouns also introduces an element of ambiguity reminiscent of the earliest section of *A Portrait of the Artist*, where "His father told him that story: his father looked at him through a glass: he had a hairy face. / He was baby tuckoo" might at first seem to imply that the hairy face belongs to baby tuckoo. Likewise, the use of the masculine pronoun in Molly Bloom's monologue is so often misleading that Shari Benstock and Bernard Benstock have devoted several pages to trying to sort out Molly's pronoun antecedents, while in *Finnegans Wake* the ambiguity of personal pronoun references is an aspect of the merging of identities within Joyce's universal dream vision.

Few readers will have more than momentary difficulty in clarifying Haines's misunderstanding, but in the same chapter Mulligan twice commits errors of interpretation that are far more difficult for the reader to spot as errors. The first comes when Mulligan takes his shaving mirror away from Stephen's face:

> —The rage of Caliban at not seeing his face in a mirror, he said. If Wilde were only alive to see you!

> Drawing back and pointing, Stephen said with bitterness:
> —It is a symbol of Irish art. The cracked lookingglass of a servant.
> (1.143–46/6)

As Thornton has demonstrated, both Mulligan and Stephen are alluding to Oscar Wilde—Mulligan to the preface to *The Picture of Dorian Gray*, Stephen to Wilde's dialogue "The Decay of Lying."[6] The dynamics of this scene might not at first be apparent, but among other things Mulligan seems intent on displaying his erudition to Stephen, and immediately refers to his source ("If Wilde were only alive to see you!") to make certain that Stephen recognizes "the rage of Caliban at not seeing his face in a mirror" as a Wildean allusion. Stephen then counters with another reference to a work by Wilde, one less well known than *Dorian Gray*, in part, perhaps, to see whether Mulligan is capable of recognizing a quotation from Wilde. That Stephen thinks of their discussion as a battle of wits is indicated by his interior monologue: "Parried again. He fears the lancet of my art as I fear that of his. The cold steel pen" (1.152–53/7). Mulligan's reply, "—Cracked lookingglass of a servant! Tell that to the oxy chap downstairs and touch him for a guinea" (1.154–55/7), might be interpreted as meaning that he thinks Haines will believe that the phrase is original, but it seems to me more likely that Mulligan himself fails to recognize Stephen's source. If so, this would suggest one reason why, when Stephen sends Mulligan a telegram later, he casts it in the form of a quotation from George Meredith's *The Ordeal of Richard Feverel* (9.550–51/199): having managed once that day to pass off a quotation as an original phrase, he wants to see if he can do it again.[7]

Mulligan's other error results from the more common sort of verbal ambiguity that we find throughout *Ulysses*. At the end of Telemachus, an unidentified swimmer tells Mulligan that he has heard from Bannon, adding that Bannon "Says he found a sweet young thing down there [Westmeath]. Photo girl he calls her," to which Mulligan replies, "—Snapshot, eh? Brief exposure" (1.684–86/21–22). Mulligan's suggestive response indicates that he misunderstands "photo girl," taking it to mean a girl who poses (perhaps scantily clad) for photographs. On a first reading, we have no reason to suspect that Mulligan has misunderstood the phrase, but later, when we read Milly's letter to Bloom (4.397–414/66), we realize that she is Bannon's "photo girl," and that the designation simply refers to the fact that she works as a clerk in a photographer's shop. Even so, the overtones that Mulligan hears in "photo girl" are not altogether irrelevant: for one thing, Milly tells Bloom that Mr. Coghlan took her picture (apparently with Mrs. Coghlan). More importantly, Mulligan's "brief exposure" is the first instance of the association of Milly with adolescent sexuality—an association that will recur in Bloom's mind throughout the day.

The most obvious examples of misunderstanding in *Ulysses* involve Bloom's inadvertent naming of a race horse, "Throwaway," and a man, "M'Intosh." The first occurs toward the end of Lotus Eaters, when Bantam Lyons scans Bloom's newspaper for information about the Ascot Gold Cup race:

> —You can keep it, Mr Bloom said.
> —Ascot. Gold cup. Wait, Bantam Lyons muttered. Half a mo. Maximum the second.
> —I was just going to throw it away, Mr Bloom said.
>   Bantam Lyons raised his eyes suddenly and leered weakly.
> —What's that? his sharp voice said.
> —I say you can keep it, Mr Bloom answered. I was going to throw it away that moment.
>   Bantam Lyons doubted an instant, leering: then thrust the outspread sheets back on Mr Bloom's arms.
> —I'll risk it, he said. Here, thanks. (5.531–41/85–86)

Bloom has no idea of the misunderstanding that has just occurred, nor is he ever enlightened as to what Lyons thinks Bloom is saying. The reader should be equally mystified at this point, but as we discover later (12.1550–57/335), Lyons believes that Bloom has given him a tip on a long shot, a horse named Throwaway. It is hard to imagine that Lyons could mistake "I was going to throw it away that moment" for a direct statement about the advisability of betting on Throwaway;

more likely, he believes that Bloom, whom many Dubliners seem to credit with possessing various kinds of inside information, is giving him a coded message. Brook Thomas has remarked that the passage provides us with "a humorous lesson about authorial intention": taking Bloom's words in a manner unintended by Bloom, Lyons proves to be "an overingenious interpreter of language." The ironies work both ways, however, for Lyons allows himself to be talked out of acting on Bloom's "tip," only to have Throwaway, a twenty-to-one outsider, win the race. As Thomas observes, "linguistic coincidence seems to have a mysterious power of prophecy."[8]

That a misinterpretation can lead to the truth is a typically Joycean irony, as is the fact that we are unlikely to trust insights arrived at in this fashion long enough to derive any benefit from them. In the newspaper account of Dignam's funeral (16.1248–61/647), the listings of Stephen Dedalus, C. P. M'Coy, and "M'Intosh" among the mourners provide us with errors, or fictions, of various orders: M'Coy is listed because Bloom passed along his request that he be included among the mourners, while Stephen's presence in the funeral story seems appropriate since Bloom reads that story while in the presence of Stephen, at the cabman's shelter. The newspaper account serves as a fiction within the larger fiction of *Ulysses,* one that rearranges events according to a certain logic. Stephen's inclusion among the mourners introduces one more point of contact with Bloom just at the moment in the novel when Bloom is hoping to build a relationship with Stephen. "C P M'Coy," meanwhile, gives us the form of the name that M'Coy stipulated when he spoke with Bloom in Lotus Eaters ("Just C. P. M'Coy will do" [5.176/76]), although the initials do not enter the conversation in which Bloom asks Hynes to put down M'Coy's name:

> —I am just taking the names, Hynes said below his breath. What is your christian name? I'm not sure.
> —L, Mr Bloom said. Leopold. And you might put down M'Coy's name too. He asked me to.
> —Charley, Hynes said writing. I know. He was on the *Freeman* once. (6.880–84/111)

A Comedy of Errors

In a novel dependent entirely upon cause-and-effect action, we might regard the change of names as an oversight on the part of the author: we would suppose he had forgotten that although M'Coy asked to be listed under his initials, Bloom had not passed along that part of the request, so that the form of the name appearing in the newspaper represents either a pure coincidence (like the inclusion of Stephen) or an authorial error. In *Ulysses,* however, the discrepancy calls for a different explanation. Without necessarily ruling out any other interpretations, we might note that the connection between M'Coy's original request and the newspaper account diverts our attention from the realistic level of action to an impression of *Ulysses* as a book in which events are manipulated and arranged rather than simply narrated and (perhaps) commented upon, as in most previous novels.

What we make of M'Intosh is another matter entirely. He enters the novel in the Hades chapter as an unknown mourner at Dignam's funeral who attracts Bloom's attention: "Now who is that lankylooking galoot over there in the macintosh? Now who is he I'd like to know? Now I'd give a trifle to know who he is" (6.805–6/109). "M'Intosh" receives his name when Hynes is taking notes for the funeral story:

> —And tell us, Hynes said, do you know that fellow in the, fellow was over there in the . . .
> He looked around.
> —Macintosh. Yes, I saw him, Mr Bloom said. Where is he now?
> —M'Intosh, Hynes said scribbling. I don't know who he is. Is that his name? (6.891–96/112)

Hynes immediately disappears—perhaps reflecting M'Intosh's mysterious appearances and disappearances—so Bloom is unable to correct the misunderstanding. Although M'Intosh is mentioned several times in later chapters, the information that we collect about him—for example, that he "loves a lady who is dead" (12.1497–98/333)—is of dubious reliability, and his identity is never revealed. Nonetheless, his "true" identity has been an irresistible subject for earnest literary sleuths who believe that Joyce's work is a "problem," which Denis Donoghue defines as "something to be solved," rather than a "mystery," that is, "something to be witnessed and attested."[9] Efforts to resolve the M'Intosh enigma seem to me as futile as the attempt to square the circle, and Herring is surely correct in regarding M'Intosh's literal identity as indeterminate.[10]

The inclusion of Stephen, M'Coy, and M'Intosh in the funeral story reminds us of the ease with which fiction can be transmuted into "history": like *Ulysses* as a whole, the article about Dignam's funeral is a composite of fact and fiction, beginning in sober realism but eventually deviating into a more extravagant variation on reality. Clive Hart and Leo Knuth have observed that in creating a book whose appearance of factual accuracy and consistency is belied by numerous errors, Joyce was reproducing some of the more prominent features of the book whose title is given in *Ulysses* as *Thom's Dublin Post Office Directory* (17.1362/708): "the volumes [of *Thom's*] published around the turn of the century often contain misprints, inconsistent spellings of the names of individuals, duplication of entries for the addresses of people who had moved during the preceding year, names of individuals who had been dead for some time."[11]

Two sorts of error stand out in the Dignam funeral story: those involving printer's errors, or "bitched type," as Bloom calls it (16.1263/648), and those involving people's names. Both kinds of error are evident in the citation of "L. Boom," a form of Bloom's name traceable, in part, to the scene in which Hynes asked for Bloom's "christian name" and Bloom initially responded "L," immediately expanding it to "Leopold" (6.880–82/111). This scene is filled with missed communication: as a Jew, Bloom obviously has no Christian name, and if he had one, it would be a full name rather than an initial. In any event, the metamorphosis of Bloom into Boom (with the absent consonant transformed into an initial: L. Boom) is only one example of changes in Bloom's name which suggest the complexity of his character and the variety of roles he plays: other examples include "Bloowho" (11.86/258), "*Booloohoom*" (15.146/434, 15.3045/538), and Bloom's own anagrams on his name:

A Comedy of Errors

Leopold Bloom
Ellpodbomool
Molldopeloob
Bollopedoom
Old Ollebo, M. P. (17.405–9/678)

These assumed or alternate identities are aspects of Bloom just as much as his pen name, "Henry Flower," which he uses in writing to Martha Clifford; they imply that in *Ulysses,* identity is not fixed or monolithic but is compounded of various elements that may surface according to circumstances. A similar, and related, ambiguity underlies Joyce's depiction of Bloom's national or ethnic identity, as we shall see later.

Errors involving names occur in *Ulysses* frequently enough to make the erroneous or indeterminate identification of characters into a theme of some significance. Looking at a flyer for a revivalist meeting, Bloom momentarily thinks he sees his own name, and a glance at a newspaper advertisement at first seems to reveal Boylan's name, but in each case Bloom is mistaken (8.8/151, 16.1238–39/647); meeting Josie Breen, he mistakenly refers to their acquaintance Mrs. Purefoy as Mrs. Beaufoy, a name suggested by Philip Beaufoy, whose *Titbits* story Bloom read in an earlier episode (8.276–79/158). Elsewhere, Bloom not only confuses Mercadante and Meyerbeer but Peter Claver (a saint) and James Carey (an informer), merging them temporarily into Peter Carey before "correcting" the name to Denis Carey (5.378–81/81); a few hours later he thinks again of "that Peter or Denis or James Carey that blew the gaff on the invincibles" (8.442–43/163), a version in which James is at least offered as one possible name for Carey. By the end of a long day, however, Bloom has reduced the possibilities to "Denis or Peter Carey" (16.1053–54/642), alternatives which not only exclude James but end with the same erroneous name that began the series.

The Cyclops narrator is often equally muddled in his references to Crofton, an Orangeman who also appears in "Ivy Day in the Committee Room": "Sure enough the castle car drove up with Martin [Cunningham] on it and Jack Power with him and a fellow named Crofter or Crofton, pensioner out of the collector general's, an orangeman Blackburn does have on the registration and he drawing his pay or Crawford gallivanting around the country at the king's expense" (12.1588–92/336). The narrator's apparent storehouse of knowledge about a man whose name he cannot get straight resembles the many rumors that circulate about Bloom in this chapter, while the fact that he is an outsider in this nationalistic company gives Crofton / Crofter / Crawford another feature in common with Bloom. Thus the inability to settle on the correct form of Crofton's name resembles the consistent misinterpretation of Bloom's character and motives as well as indicating the extent of Crofton's own estrangement from the pub society. The narrator's initial alternatives of "Crofter or Crofton . . . or Crawford" give way to "Crofter the Orangeman or presbyterian" (12.1634/337) and "Crofton or Crawford" (12.1752/341), before the narrator describes Bloom's hasty departure from Barney Kiernan's pub in the company of Martin Cunningham, Jack Power, and "Crofton or whatever you call him" (12.1768–69/341).

In *Ulysses*, errors in references to names are generally significant, but each instance is not necessarily meaningful in the same manner as others. Molly Bloom's confusion of *alias* and *Ananias* (17.686–87/686) has a logic of its own, since an alias is a false name while Ananias was a speaker of falsehoods; Bantam Lyons's misunderstanding of Bloom's "I was just going to throw it away" not only leads to a valid (if unintended) tip on a horse but suggests a correspondence between Throwaway and Bloom, another dark horse or outsider; and the inadvertent naming of M'Intosh demonstrates the ease with which fictitious identities might be created in a modern, impersonal society. Other sorts of errors also point to the fallibility of the human agents responsible for the mistakes. Typographical or printer's errors, for instance, have the effect of demystifying the printed text by calling attention to the human, and therefore fallible, agent behind the text, as when Bloom sees the "line of bitched type" in the funeral story and attributes it to the foreman's having distracted the typesetter (16.1257–59/647; compare this with 7.180–90/121–22). Stephen's recollection of "a blue French telegram, curiosity to show," reading "Nother dying come home father" (3.197–99/42), implies the existence of a French telegraph operator whose inadequate English led him to mistranscribe the intended "Mother" as "Nother," while Martha Clifford's famous mistakes—"I called you naughty boy because I do not like that other world," "if you do not wrote," and "before my patience are exhausted" (5.244–54/77–78)—tell us that we are dealing with an inexperienced typist whose grasp of English grammar may be as weak as her proofreading ability.

That we are to pay attention to these errors is suggested by the fact that Stephen and Bloom do so: the "curiosity" of Stephen's telegram lies precisely in the erroneous "Nother," while Bloom not only notes the printer's errors in the funeral account but calls our attention to Martha's "if you do not wrote" by thinking, ironically, "Wonder did she wrote it herself" (5.268–69/78). The transformation of "write" into "wrote" can easily be attributed to the fact that "i" and "o" are adjacent on Martha's typewriter, but changing "word" into "world" would have been harder to do, especially with a manual typewriter that would not have responded easily to chance contact with a key. My suspicion is that Martha's three mistakes are of three distinct orders: a simple typing error (write/ wrote); a grammatical mistake caused by an attempt to sound educated (patience are/ patience is); and a typing error caused by a momentary hesitation between two words (word/ world), one distinguished from the other by the addition of a phallic "l" just as Bloom will be reduced to Boom by the deletion of the same letter.

The opportunities for interpretation of Martha's *word/ world* mistake are abundant, and there is little point in attempting to exhaust them here. As a final example of the way error can lead to truths that might not otherwise be accessible, however, we might briefly look at Bloom's later recollections of this single error. Bloom thinks of Martha's "I called you naughty boy because I do not like that other world" in the Hades, Lestrygonians, and Sirens episodes (6.1002–1003/115, 8.327–28/160, 11.871/279), and in each instance the reference is thematically significant. Bloom's final allusion to the letter passage comes in the Nausicaa chapter, near the end, as Bloom attempts to write a message in the sand:

> Mr Bloom with his stick gently vexed the thick sand at his foot. Write a message for her. Might remain. What?
> I.
> Some flatfoot tramp on it in the morning. Useless. Washed away. Tide comes here. Saw a pool near her foot. Bend, see my face there, dark mirror, breathe on it, stirs. All these rocks with lines and scars and letters. O, those transparent! Besides they don't know. *What is the meaning of that other world. I called you naughty boy because I do not like.*
> AM. A.
> No room. Let it go.
> Mr Bloom effaced the letters with his slow boot. (13.1256–66/ 381; emphasis added)

Much commentary has been expended upon Bloom's incomplete message, and it is generally agreed that there is no way to know for certain how the sentence would have ended. Without precluding other interpretations, however, we might entertain the possibility that Bloom intends to duplicate a sentence that he used in a letter to Martha, a sentence ending with a word that Martha does not recognize (or pretends not to recognize), although she realizes that it signifies unorthodox sexual taste, since she euphemizes it into "naughty boy." The fact that Martha refers more than once to her desire to punish Bloom suggests that Bloom has invited those references in his letter, so that the word most likely to lie behind Martha's "naughty boy" may well be *masochist*. If this is what Bloom is thinking of, however, its length prevents him from finishing his sentence in the sand ("No room. Let it go"), so that whatever our speculations, we cannot say with certainty that Bloom is thinking of one particular word.

As Paul van Caspel has shown in his book *Bloomers on the Liffey*, it is easy to misread *Ulysses*, easy to fall into error. What are commonly called "reader traps" may be found throughout the book, and it is humbling for seasoned readers to recall the errors that they made in

A Comedy of Errors

their earliest encounters with the text: for example, assuming that
when the barmaids in Sirens chortle over the possibility of being married to a chemist from Boyd's pharmacy, the narrator's interpolated
"Married to Bloom, to greaseabloom" (11.180/260) indicates that
the women were speaking of Bloom; or that Bloom's "I have such a
bad headache today" (13.778–79/368) means that Bloom has a headache, whereas he is merely recalling a phrase from Martha's letter; or
that "There's eleven of them," shouted at the end of Oxen of the Sun
(14.1562/427), refers to bar patrons rather than clock strokes. If our
own fallibility is one of the book's subjects, however, another is the
inadequacy of any single viewpoint, or system, or conception of the
truth, or for that matter any single interpretive stance that we might
take toward Ulysses. Error and its companion, rumor, which I will
discuss in the next chapter, are essential aspects of Joyce's grand human vision, one that embraces the comedy of life with a zest rarely
encountered in the literature of any age.

6 ——

Dublin Alligators

> So in comes Martin asking where was Bloom.
> —Where is he? says Lenehan. Defrauding widows and orphans.
> —Isn't that a fact, says John Wyse, what I was telling the citizen
> about Bloom and the Sinn Fein?
> —That's so, says Martin. Or so they allege.
> —Who made those allegations? says Alf.
> —I, says Joe. I'm the alligator. (12.1621–27/337)

In June 1921, less than a year before the publication of *Ulysses*, Joyce wrote to his benefactor Harriet Shaw Weaver that "A nice collection could be made of legends about me." Among the rumors that had reached his ears were stories that he had spied "for one or both combatants" during the world war; that he was a cocaine addict; that he had had a nervous breakdown and had gone to New York, where he was near death; that he owned movie houses in Switzerland; that he was either "almost blind, emaciated and consumptive" or "an austere mixture of the Dalai Lama and sir Rabindranath Tagore"; and that he "always carried four watches and rarely spoke except to ask my neighbour what o'clock it was" (Ellmann 510). Earlier rumors, which

Dublin Alligators

Joyce passed along in a letter to Stanislaus, had him spying "in Dublin for the Austrians, in Zurich for the British or for the Sinn Feiners," or associated him in various ways with Dadaism, Bolshevism, and various nobility, including the Dowager Empress of China (Ellmann 509). Although Joyce defended himself against one rumor—that he was too lazy to accomplish anything—by calculating the number of hours that he had spent writing *Ulysses*, and expressed some irritation at the idea that he needed psychiatric help, he appeared generally to accept rumors as inevitable. Living in Ireland, where rumor-mongering is so much a way of life that Hugh Kenner has coined the term "Irish Fact" to refer to the sort of rumors preferred there, Joyce would have been accustomed both to the assumption that rumors are an unavoidable aspect of life and to the tendency for people to cling to their "unfacts," as he calls them in *Finnegans Wake* (57.16).

Myth and history, gossip and gospel, are essentially inseparable in *Finnegans Wake*, where words like "fact(s)" and "factual" appear with surprising frequency, given that it is all "a matter of fict" (532.14–15). In *Ulysses*, where we at least have a basis for separating some facts from their corresponding unfacts, there are numerous examples of rumors that are demonstrably untrue. Lenehan's statement that Bloom is off "defrauding widows and orphans," for instance, is not only false, it is precisely the opposite of the truth, since Bloom is at that moment arranging for the payment of Paddy Dignam's life insurance benefits to his widow and orphans. As Kenner has noted, however, there *is* an element of fraud in the transaction, although the widow and orphans are to be the beneficiaries rather than the victims of the maneuver: Dignam used the insurance policy as collateral for a loan that he never repaid, and only a technicality that Bloom is willing to exploit—Dignam's failure to notify the insurance company of the transaction—prevents the moneylender, Bridgeman, from collecting the insurance money as payment on the debt.[1] In his own muddled way, Bloom explains the technicality earlier in the Cyclops episode (12.760 ff./313), and the dubious morality of the ploy might well be one reason why the narrator recalls another time when Bloom was

53

supposed to have skated on thin ice: Bloom, the narrator recalls, "was bloody safe he wasn't run in himself under the act that time as a rogue and vagabond only he had a friend in court. Selling bazaar tickets or what do you call it royal Hungarian privileged lottery. True as you're there. O, commend me to an israelite! Royal and privileged Hungarian robbery" (12.775–79 / 313).

Unlike the narrator, Lenehan was not present when Bloom tried to explain what he was doing about the insurance payment, and his allegation of fraud comes as a reflexive act of anti-Semitic nastiness. The fact that he gets one thing almost right—that Bloom is involved in a morally dubious action—is typical of the way rumors work in *Ulysses*, although it is equally typical that Lenehan gets the main point wrong (Bloom acts out of kindness and altruism, not greed). Lenehan is busy elaborating on a rumor that he started a few moments earlier: that Bloom "had a few bob on *Throwaway* and he's gone to gather in the shekels" (12.1550–51 / 335). The reference to "shekels" tells us why Lenehan is so eager to spread this rumor of Bloom's wealth, but since a precise sum of money always makes a more credible rumor than an indeterminate one, Lenehan immediately converts the shekels to more familiar currency: "Bet you what you like he has a hundred shillings to five on. He's the only man in Dublin has it" (15.1555–56 / 335).

Lenehan's assurance conspires with Bloom's status as an outsider and the alcoholic atmosphere of the gathering to confirm the amount of the bet in the mind of the narrator, who thinks it would be "justifiable homicide" to kill Bloom for "sloping off with his five quid without putting up a pint of stuff like a man" (12.1662–63 / 338). Within minutes the narrator irritably sees Bloom's rumored actions as confirmation of a Jewish stereotype: "There's a jew for you!" he thinks; "All for number one. Cute as a shithouse rat. Hundred to five " (12.1760–61 / 341). In Circe, the nameless narrator reappears briefly to snarl, "Arse over tip. Hundred shillings to five" (15.1149 / 470). Like Lenehan's other rumor about Bloom, however, this one has at least a tangential relationship to reality: Bloom's trip to the courthouse is indeed related to five shillings that he put down, but the shillings were a contribution to a fund for the Dignam family (10.974–80/246, 11.805/277, 11.866/279, 17.1462/711). Since Lenehan knew nothing of this contribution, the slim correspondence between rumor and reality is a matter of pure coincidence; most likely, the five bob that Lenehan says Bloom wagered on Throwaway is simply transferred from Bantam Lyons, who planned to bet that sum (8.1016/179) until Lenehan talked him out of it.

Among the rumors that can be safely assumed to have no factual basis is the legend that Parnell is still alive and will return to save his people (6.923–24/112, 16.1297–1306/648–49), a rumor parallel to today's tabloid stories about Elvis Presley. Then again, presumably dead people do turn out to be alive in John M. Synge's plays *In the Shadow of the Glen* and *The Playboy of the Western World*, in Lady Gregory's *Spreading the News*, and for that matter in the song "Finnegan's Wake," from which Joyce derived the title of his last book. People thought likely to be dead return, with a vengeance, in *The Odyssey* and *The Count of Monte Cristo;* the plots of *Oedipus Rex*, *The Winter's Tale*, and "Rip Van Winkle" also turn upon the unexpected survival of key characters. Given that one of the central themes of *Ulysses* is the return, it stands to reason that there will be numerous variations on the motif, and that these would overlap one another: Bloom's thought that "in nine cases out of ten" someone who returns, after being thought dead, lives in "complete oblivion because it was twenty odd years" (16.1308–10/649) establishes a connection between Odysseus and other men who are not recognized after a twenty-year absence.[2] In any event, Parnell, who probably won't return, and the untrustworthy sailor D. B. Murphy, who has returned (possibly using an alias, since he is carrying a postcard addressed to A. Boudin—16.489/626, 16.1235/647), are variations both on the homeward-bound Bloom and on his Homeric counterpart.

Paralleling (and caricaturing) the myth of Parnell's return is the inadvertently generated story of Paddy Dignam's return. Even amidst the numerous references to resurrection in *Ulysses*, it is startling to hear Alf Bergan say, in response to an inquiry about Willy Murray, "I

saw him just now in Capel street with Paddy Dignam" (12.314–15/
300). Confronted with the fact of Paddy Dignam's death, Alf prefers
to trust his own senses:

> —Sure I'm after seeing him not five minutes ago, says Alf, as plain
> as a pikestaff.
> —Who's dead? says Bob Doran.
> —You saw his ghost then, says Joe, God between us and harm.
> —What? says Alf. Good Christ, only five. . . . What? . . . And Willy
> Murray with him, the two of them there near whatdoyou-
> callhim's. . . . What? Dignam dead?
> —What about Dignam? says Bob Doran. Who's talking about . . . ?
> —Dead! says Alf. He's no more dead than you are.
> —Maybe so, says Joe. They took the liberty of burying him this
> morning anyhow. (12.323–33/300–1)

Appropriately enough, Joe Hynes, who debunks the story that Dignam
is alive, made a visit that morning to Parnell's grave, and in response to
Mr. Power's statement that "Some say he is not in that grave at all. That
the coffin was filled with stones. That one day he will come again,"
remarked sorrowfully, "Parnell will never come again. . . . He's there,
all that was mortal of him" (6.923–27/112–13). If the legend that
Parnell will return establishes the Irish politician as a version of Odysseus, Alf Bergan's account of Paddy Dignam's continued existence
might be regarded as a comic version of the Parnell myth.

The passage also points to the double nature of reality in *Ulysses*:
people who are not physically present exist, for us, only in our imagina-
tions, and in Alf Bergan's mind Paddy Dignam has continued to exist for
an extended time after ceasing to live for other people. The sense of
double realities is pressed home by the presence in this passage of Willy
Murray, a character who is mentioned nowhere else in *Ulysses*, but who
apparently would be known to Joe Hynes and other members of Alf
Bergan's crowd. Murray lends his first name to Paddy Dignam a page
later as the drunken Bob Doran mourns the death of "poor little Willy
Dignam" and immediately launches into a panegyric on Dignam—

Willy or Paddy—as "the finest man . . . the finest purest character" (12.388–96 / 302).

That Dignam is subject to unexpected resurrection, a change of name, and a startling improvement in his reputation is remarkable enough, but it is also striking to see him paired with Willy Murray. As Richard Ellmann has shown, the real William Murray was James Joyce's uncle, and in *Ulysses* he appears frequently under the name Richie Goulding (Ellmann 19–20, 45). It seems somehow appropriate that Willy Murray would surface in Alf Bergan's mind in the company of an ambulant Paddy Dignam, for Murray and Goulding are the real-life and fictional variants on the same person, just as Paddy Dignam (in the grave) and Paddy / Willy Dignam (walking about the streets) exist on two distinct levels of reality. The logic may extend one step further, if Robert Adams is correct in his belief that Dignam was based largely on John Joyce's friend Matthew Kane.[3] Kane, as Ellmann tells us, was also the model for Martin Cunningham, so in the Hades chapter he contributes aspects of his identity both to Dignam and to one of his mourners. Kane will reappear a third time, under his own name, in the Ithaca chapter: asking what Bloom thinks about after Stephen leaves him, the narrator answers that he is reminded "of companions now in various manners in different places defunct," including one "Matthew F. Kane (accidental drowning, Dublin Bay)" as well as "Patrick Dignam (apoplexy, Sandymount)" (17.1249–55 / 704–5). The Matthew F. Kane named here is not precisely the one Joyce knew, however, for that Kane drowned in Dublin Bay in July 1904, so that a month earlier, when *Ulysses* takes place, Bloom could not be thinking of his death. The historical Kane, in effect, exists here in three forms: as Dignam, as Cunningham, and as another person with the same name and fate (but a somewhat different chronology) living in the parallel universe of Joyce's book.

These metamorphoses of identity juxtapose variations upon the same person: the Bloom of our imagination, who gave five shillings to a good cause, against Lenehan's Bloom, who turned a five-shilling bet into a huge profit and now keeps his winnings a secret to avoid having to buy a round of drinks; the historical Parnell, who is in the grave, against the mythic Parnell, whose coffin was filled with stones; the Paddy Dignam whom they took the liberty of burying against the one who runs about with Willy Murray; the William Murray and Matthew Kane who gave their identities, in large part, to fictional characters with other names, against the Murray and Kane who have cameo roles under their own names. Similarly, rumors, which give us an example of the creative imagination at work, are alternate forms of reality, the kind created in an oral culture where conversation is one of the most highly developed forms of art. Rumors become a problem for the reader of *Ulysses* because in banishing the nineteenth-century omniscient narrator, who could be trusted to separate fact from rumor, Joyce throws the responsibility for evaluating rumors back on the reader without providing us with any final adjudication of our verdicts. Since much of what happens in *Ulysses* is what people say and think about one another, it is obviously important for us to know whether or not Joyce's gossips know whereof they speak. Unfortunately, it is easier to begin rumors than to verify them, and sometimes it is impossible to decide whether or not they are true without more evidence.

The ease with which one might start a rumor may be illustrated by a scene in Eumaeus, a chapter filled with unverifiable stories. Overhearing talk of Kitty O'Shea—"That bitch, that English whore," as one character calls her (16.1352/650)—Bloom offers the suggestion that she was a passionate woman since "if I don't greatly mistake she was Spanish too" (16.1412–13/652). Bloom *is* greatly mistaken, however, since Mrs. O'Shea was not Spanish: Bloom is probably assuming such a strong parallel between his adulterous wife and Kitty O'Shea that he is ready to see other parallels as well, even when they don't exist. In any event, Bloom's reference to Spain leads Stephen to call Kitty O'Shea "the king of Spain's daughter," meaning that like the princess in the nursery rhyme "I Had a Little Nut Tree," she is brought across the water to see something miraculous, in this case Charles Stewart Parnell. Bloom takes Stephen's allusion literally,[4] and responds, "Was she? . . . I never heard that rumour before. Possible, especially there, it was as she lived there. So, Spain" (16.1414–20/ 652). Here, it is simple enough for readers to discount the "rumour," since we have seen how it was generated out of Bloom's failure to recognize Stephen's ironic reference to a nursery rhyme.

There are, of course, rumors that even the gossip-hungry Dubliners of *Ulysses* refuse to give full credence. Martin Cunningham attempts to squelch one rumor, that Bloom is "a cousin of Bloom the dentist" (12.1638–41/337). This is an understandable error, one probably made by many readers of *Ulysses* who see Cashel Boyle O'Connor Fitzmaurice Tisdall Farrell stride "past Mr Bloom's dental windows" in the Wandering Rocks chapter (10.1115/250): since this is the first mention of the dentist, readers are likely to assume either that our Bloom is or has been a dentist, or that the reference is to the office where Bloom's dentist is located, or that the passage refers to another Bloom, probably a relative. Cunningham's firmness in denying the rumor that Bloom is related to the dentist gives him an air of authority, which may be why some readers readily accept Cunningham's confirmation of John Wyse Nolan's assertion that "it was Bloom gave the ideas for Sinn Fein to Griffith to put in his paper," even though Cunningham immediately follows his assured "That's so" with a cautious "Or so they allege" (12.1573 ff./335–37). We might note that Cunningham has just assented to a rumor without knowing exactly what he is confirming, since Nolan aired the story of Bloom and Sinn Fein before Cunningham entered the pub; and if we recall that Cunningham is just as certain of his "facts" in the *Dubliners* story "Grace," where he passes on a good deal of misinformation about Catholic church history and theology, we might be more skeptical of his statements about Bloom's involvement with Arthur Griffith. It is true that Bloom has had some brief connection with Sinn Fein advocates, if we can believe Molly Bloom's recollection that "he was going about with some of them Sinner Fein lately or whatever they call themselves talking his usual trash and nonsense . . . still it must have been him he knew there was a boycott" (18.383–87/748). Nonetheless, it is hard to imagine the anti-Semitic Griffith, who presented his

Sinn Fein ("ourselves") policy of Irish economic self-sufficiency in the pages of his paper, the *United Irishman,* taking advice from Leopold Bloom.

The most likely source of this rumor is another of Cunningham's allegations, that Bloom is "a perverted jew . . . from a place in Hungary and it was he drew up all the plans according to the Hungarian system. We know that in the castle" (12.1635–37/337). Bloom, of course, is not from Hungary: only a few minutes earlier, when he was asked what his country was, Bloom answered, "Ireland. . . . I was born here" (12.1431/331). Bloom's Hungarian connection is simply a matter of ancestry, and whatever he knows about "the Hungarian system" of organizing opposition to foreign rule he has probably learned where everyone else in Dublin would be reading about it, in the pages of the *United Irishman,* where Griffith's *The Resurrection of Hungary* was serialized from January to June 1904. Being given to involvement in political discussions, Bloom would be heard talking about Sinn Fein, his Hungarian ancestry would be recalled, and in Dublin the result would be a rumor. Bloom's status as a figure on the margins of Dublin middle-class society, which makes him a mysterious character for his fellow citizens, would contribute to the spreading of such a rumor. Another contributing factor undoubtedly is Martin Cunningham's eagerness to make himself seem important by association with someone responsible for one of the major political events of the day, even though he has to cite Dublin Castle, the center of British political power in Ireland, as his source of information about the development of an anti-British political platform.

Some of the *Ulysses* rumors are clearly untrue (Bloom did not win a hundred shillings on Throwaway, and Paddy Dignam was not walking about the streets several hours after his funeral); others are highly improbable (Bloom is unlikely to have been heavily involved in Sinn Fein, much less to have been one of its founding fathers). Other rumors might or might not be true. The story of Corley's alleged descent from nobility, told by Stephen to Bloom (16.130–43/616), is impossible to confirm, although if true the rumor might affect our reading of "Two Gallants," where Corley makes his previous appearance as a decidedly ungallant seducer. Likewise, it is wonderful to contemplate the possibility that the jingoistic Citizen has been threatened by the Molly Maguires "for grabbing the holding of an evicted tenant" (12.1312–16/328), since this would undercut much of his talk about British exploitation of the Irish; but since the source is the Cyclops narrator, who has hardly a good word to say about anyone, the rumor cannot be confirmed. The narrator likewise peddles the story of Bob Doran's drunken encounter with two streetwalkers who picked his pockets: this rumor, passed along on the authority of Paddy Leonard, has the ring of truth about it, but the fact that it is immediately followed by a somewhat exaggerated version of how Doran was entrapped into marriage (the standard account may be found in the *Dubliners* story "The Boarding House") might well weaken our confidence in all the Doran rumors.

In the category of undecidable rumors we probably should also place the story that the proprietor of the cabman's shelter, in Eumaeus, is the James Fitzharris—nicknamed Skin-the-Goat—who was one of the drivers involved in the Phoenix Park murders of 1882. In the Aeolus chapter the rumor is introduced virtually as an established fact: "—Skin-the-Goat, Mr O'Madden Burke said. Fitzharris. He has that cabman's shelter, they say, down there at Butt bridge. Holohan told me. You know Holohan?" (7.641–43/136). We do know Hoppy Holohan: he is the person who told M'Coy about Paddy Dignam's death (5.95–129/73–74). Known here and in "Two Gallants" as a pub-crawler, appearing in "A Mother" as the inept organizer of a recital for the Eire Abu Society, Holohan is not the sort of person on whose rumors you would risk your life, even if he does correctly report the fact of Dignam's death. The phrase "they say" is even more troublesome, implying as it does that even O'Madden Burke realizes he is merely passing along a common rumor. And when we return to Skin-the-Goat in the Eumaeus episode, Bloom is even more explicit in distancing himself from the story: "Mr Bloom and Stephen entered the cabman's shelter, an unpretentious wooden structure, where, prior to then, he had rarely if ever been before, the former having previously whispered to the latter a few hints anent the keeper of it said to be the once famous Skin-the-Goat, Fitzharris, the invincible, though he could not vouch for the actual facts which quite possibly there was not one vestige of truth in" (16.320–25 / 621).

Bloom's doubts grow: he connects "the licensee of the place rumoured to be or have been Fitzharris, the famous invincible," with the "obviously bogus" sailor D. B. Murphy, and considers the possibility that the two are involved in a "confidence trick"; he guesses that "the lessee or keeper . . . probably wasn't the other person at all"; he recalls that "Fitz, nicknamed Skin-the, merely drove the car for the actual perpetrators of the outrage" (an error on Bloom's part, by the way: Fitzharris drove a decoy car, not the one in which the "actual perpetrators" rode); and finally he thinks of the keeper as "our friend, the pseudo Skin-the-etcetera" (16.1043–70 / 641–42). Bloom's skepticism about the whole affair puts us on guard, but it hardly resolves matters, and the question of the shelter keeper's identity is left uncertain as Bloom and Stephen leave for Bloom's house.

Further rumors might easily be generated, and in Circe and Ithaca we are given examples of a genre that we might call second-level, or potential, rumors: rumors that could be created but at present don't necessarily exist as such because we cannot point to a particular character who believes in them. The list of Molly Bloom's "lovers," concocted by the Ithacan catechist as an exercise in setting up a catalogue of the possible occupants of Molly's bed, is such a potential rumor (17.2132–42 / 731). Over the years, as critics have become increasingly skeptical in their examination of Joycean evidence, the assumption that the catalogue is quite literally a list of men with whom Molly has had affairs has given way to the alternative suggestion that the catalogue merely reflects Bloom's suspicions that Molly has had (or might have had) affairs with these men. Yet a careful reading indicates that the list lacks even the sanction of Bloom's imagination. The narrator, after all, asks "If [Bloom] had smiled why would he have smiled?" (17.2126 / 731); and having said that he would have smiled at the thought that "each one who enters [Molly's bed] imagines himself to be the first to enter whereas he is always the last term of a preceding series even if the first term of a succeeding one," goes on to develop the series that the apparently unsmiling Bloom would have been thinking about had he in fact smiled. In another version of *Ulysses* in which Bloom not only smiled but then thought of the rather improbable series of lovers, that series might easily have the status of a rumor, but here it is essentially divorced from reality, serving only to suggest one of the many possible perspectives on Molly Bloom, seen here as a woman whose sexual adventures reach toward infinity.

The "hallucinations" of Circe, as the more extravagant actions of that episode are often called, might well serve a similar function: not precisely rumors, they are parodies of rumors, so exaggerated that nobody could believe them (although readers often assume that the surreal sequences have a less direct relationship to literal reality). No reader, I suspect, actually believes that Bloom has *"eight male yellow and white children,"* even though the text assures us that this is so, adding that *"All the octuplets are handsome, with valuable metallic faces, wellmade, respectably dressed and wellconducted, speaking five modern languages fluently and interested in various arts and sciences"* (15.1821–26/494). Even such an event has antecedents in the earlier, more "realistic," chapters of *Ulysses*. The theme of male pregnancy is first introduced by Stephen Dedalus in the Scylla and Charybdis chapter, as part of his Shakespeare theory: John Shakespeare, according to Stephen, "rests, disarmed of fatherhood, having devised that mystical estate upon his son. Boccaccio's Calandrino was the first and last man who felt himself with child. Fatherhood, in the sense of conscious begetting, is unknown to man" (9.835–38/207). Calandrino, in Boccaccio's *Decameron*, is duped into thinking he is pregnant and then is "cured" after spending a good deal of money on worthless medicines, so the point here is that male pregnancy does not exist. When Stephen goes on to refer to the Sabellian heresy that "the Father was Himself His Own Son," Mulligan parodies the idea by proclaiming himself pregnant with a play in his brain and clasping "his paunchbrow with both birthaiding hands" (9.862–78/208); by the end of the chapter, Mulligan has further degraded Stephen's theory into a fantasy of masturbation (9.1170 ff./216–17). The fact that Mulligan and Stephen immediately encounter Bloom (9.1197 ff./217) may suggest why in

Oxen of the Sun, when Mulligan again meets Bloom, he asks him whether he has come to the maternity hospital for "professional assistance," implying that Bloom might be pregnant (14.721/403). Dr. Dixon immediately transfers the joke back to Mulligan, inquiring into the reason for his enlarged stomach, but in Circe it is Dixon who proclaims that Bloom is expecting a baby.

Throughout the Cyclops chapter, one of the recurrent slurs against Bloom is that he is too feminine to be a real man. When Bloom says that Boylan is "an excellent man to organise"—falling prey to the same slip of the tongue that he made earlier, in Davy Byrne's (8.797/173)—the narrator immediately picks up the implication: "Hoho begob says I to myself says I. That explains the milk in the cocoanut and absence of hair on the animal's chest. Blazes doing the tootle on the flute. . . . That's the bucko that'll organise her, take my tip. 'Twixt me and you Caddareesh" (12.995–1002/319). The Citizen surely means to include Bloom along with Denis Breen as "a half and half," a "fellow that's neither fish nor flesh," a "pishogue" (12.1052–58/321), and Bloom's championship of love as the supreme virtue hardly wins any sympathy from the Citizen, who immediately brands Bloom "a nice pattern of a Romeo and Juliet" (12.1492/333). By the time the conversation reaches Bloom's history as a father, the general resentment of him, possibly abetted by a stereotype of Jews as effeminate men, culminates in a series of insults to Bloom's virility: the Citizen sneers at the idea that Bloom would buy baby food for Rudy and, told that Bloom's wife had two children, rasps, "And who does he suspect?"; Joe Hynes wonders "did he ever put it out of sight"—a particularly appropriate metaphor for intercourse in a chapter dominated by references to vision and blindness; and the narrator, who regards Bloom as "one of those mixed middlings," recalls Pisser Burke's story of Bloom "lying up in the hotel . . . once a month with headache like a totty with her courses" (12.1650–60/338). As improbable as it sounds, that last story has at least an element of truth in it, for Molly's recollection at the outset of the Penelope chapter is that Bloom hasn't asked for breakfast in bed "since the City Arms hotel when he used to be pretending to be laid up with a sick voice doing his highness to make himself interesting for that old faggot Mrs Riordan that he thought he had a great leg of and she never left us a farthing" (18.2–5 / 738). Left to decide between the narrator's story of a menstruating Bloom and Molly's recollection of Bloom's feigning illness to arouse the sympathy of a supposedly rich woman, we surely opt for Molly's version, but on another level the narrator's conception of Bloom fits rather well with Molly's subsequent admission that Bloom "understood or felt what a woman is" (18.1579 / 782).

Like Bloom's pregnancy, the other fantasies of Circe have this in common with the rumors that circulate throughout *Ulysses:* not literally true, they have a skewed or figurative relationship to the truth, representing perspectives on the characters and actions that are not controlled by the ordinary laws of time, space, biological makeup, or narrative logic. And their fundamentally undecidable status, as they seem to be located neither in the minds of specific characters nor in that of a definable narrator, means that their relationship to the literal action can never be stated with absolute assurance, so that we can no more dismiss them as having no bearing on Bloom and Stephen than we can accept them as direct manifestations of those characters' conscious or unconscious desires.

In her highly interesting study of the literary uses of gossip, Patricia Meyer Spacks connects the act of reading with gossip, noting that "what reader and narrator share is a set of responses to the private doings of richly imagined individuals."[5] The voyeuristic element implied by Spacks's comparison is precisely what George Russell finds objectionable in Stephen's *Hamlet* theory, which consists of "this prying into the family life of a great man" (9.181 / 189). Readers of novels spend their time prying into the lives of fictional characters, and the result, normally, is that we reach a point at which we know what the author, or the narrator, knows about the characters. Spacks describes the situation in *Emma*, which seems to me a representative example of the traditional novel: under the narrator's guidance, the reader participates in the gossip of Highbury, formulates new interpretations as more "raw material for interpretation, the raw material of gossip" comes forth, and ultimately recognizes the inadequacy of all previous interpretations (rumors) to account for the facts as they are finally known.[6] What we know, of course, is essentially what Emma knows, so at the end of the novel we have at our disposal essentially the same facts that Emma has. In *Ulysses*, however, the situation is different: as Michael Seidel has noted, "*Ulysses* is so designed that its participants never learn very much about the plot they are in."[7] Moreover, in *Emma*, our final assurance that we can distinguish truth from rumor, fact from fiction, is made possible by the presence throughout the novel of a single narrator whose presentation and evaluation of the facts cannot be second-guessed. By contrast, in *Ulysses* there is no single privileged point of view but rather a series of viewpoints that are limited in various ways; moreover, while we end the novel knowing some things that Bloom does not know, Bloom knows other things that we don't. That we can discount some rumors and qualify others with assurance is due to the realistic core of *Ulysses;* that other rumors cannot be either confirmed or disproved is the result of Joyce's rejection of omniscience and narrative closure, the two elements that in more conventional novels are closely associated with the resolution of competing interpretations of the facts.

For readers, this means living with uncertainty, with mystery. We do not know who sent Denis Breen a postcard reading either "U.P." or "U.p.: up," depending on whether we assume that Bloom reads the entire postcard or only part of it (8.257–58/158); Bloom suspects either Alf Bergan or Richie Goulding (8.320/160), and Bergan's delight in the situation might suggest that he is involved, but we have no hard evidence of his complicity. Much less do we know for certain how to interpret the postcard, although we might be inclined to believe that the enigmatic message has no meaning at all and is simply intended to torment Breen by holding out the possibility of a meaning that cannot be pinpointed or confirmed. The opinion that *Ulysses* is a hoax was shared by a number of early reviewers of the book, and while few today would argue that the book is essentially nonsense, it is true that it rejects, at every turn, the idea of a fixed, determinate meaning. Narrated in a variety of styles that suggest the impossibility of viewing its events from a single perspective, *Ulysses* resists our attempts to resolve all its ambiguities, to reduce it to one set of facts or to a single level of meaning. And just as the most interesting perspectives, errors, and rumors find their locus in Bloom, so the book's crucial question of ethnic, national, or racial identity—a question as plagued by ambiguity as any of the events of the book—revolves primarily about Bloom's multiple identifications as Irishman, Jew, and Greek hero.

7 ——

An Epic of Two Races

The theme of national, ethnic, or racial identity is almost constantly before us in *Ulysses*, as Joyce examines the assumptions underlying our attitudes toward different groups. Early in the first chapter, for example, Buck Mulligan calls attention to the classical (and therefore non-Irish) form of the name "Dedalus": "—The mockery of it! he said gaily. Your absurd name, an ancient Greek!" (1.34/3). This remark might well be in Stephen's mind much later, in the Eumaeus chapter, when the sailor D. B. Murphy calls Simon Dedalus "All Irish" and Stephen answers, "All too Irish" (16.383–84/623). Stephen, who vowed at the end of *A Portrait* to "forge . . . the uncreated conscience of [his] race," knew even then that "the shortest way to Tara was *via* Holyhead" (250, 253). Tara was the ancient meetingplace for the kings of Ireland, and Holyhead, in Wales, was a place where boats from Dublin and Kingstown would take their passengers. Thus Stephen's comment signifies that only by leaving Ireland, or escaping narrow conceptions of racial or cultural identity, could the Irish writer gain the breadth of vision needed to develop a valid identity for twentieth century Ireland.

An Epic of Two Races

Mulligan's comment about the name Dedalus is not the first reference to the ways names reveal the blurring of national identities, for the book's title does not give us *Odysseus* but *Ulysses,* a Roman transformation of a Greek name. Indeed, when we look at the title of *Ulysses* we might first echo Leopold Bloom's assessment that the word *metempsychosis* is "Greek," followed by his more accurate description of the word as "from the Greek" (4.341/64). Joyce could have selected *Ulysses* over *Odysseus* simply because the Roman form was more common in post-Homeric accounts of Odysseus: Virgil, Dante, Shakespeare, and Tennyson all called the Greek warrior Ulysses, as did Charles Lamb in *The Adventures of Ulysses,* the book in which Joyce first encountered his favorite hero. A more subtle reason, however, is that the Latinized Greek name points to the ambiguity of national and cultural identity, a problem that is one of the central themes of *Ulysses.*

I noted in chapter 1 that *Ulysses* was written during a time of intense debate about Irish identity. Although Joyce at one time supported Arthur Griffith's Sinn Fein policies, which called for a boycott of English goods, he never gave his allegiance fully or blindly to any political cause—as we might see from a 1906 letter to Stanislaus in which Joyce complained that Griffith's paper was "educating the people of Ireland on the old pap of racial hatred" (*Letters* 2:167). In *Ulysses,* Joyce explored the questions of cultural identity raised by the Gaelic Revival, the Irish Literary Renaissance, and the demand for Irish political independence from Great Britain. That his protagonist was an Irish Jew of Hungarian descent—and figuratively the reincarnation of a Greek hero—might on its face be regarded as a critique of the Irish parochialism that Joyce had battled ever since "The Day of the Rabblement." The critique goes deeper, however, for at every turn *Ulysses* violates the boundaries that separate people and shows the inadequacy of the language that we use to describe national or ethnic groups. And nowhere is that critique more penetrating than in its exploration of Bloom's ambiguous status as a Jew.

LEOPOLD BLOOM AS AUTHENTIC JEW

Joyce told Carlo Linati that *Ulysses* was "an epic of two races (Israelite-Irish)" (*Letters* 1:146). That formulation omits the Greeks, whose role in the symbolic action of *Ulysses* is so important that Joyce insisted that the first edition have a blue and white cover in honor of the Greek flag. Odysseus is the prototypical wandering hero whose return home prefigures Leopold Bloom's; similarly, the Greek respect for pure intelligence resurfaces in Bloom's active and penetrating mind. Nonetheless, the two ethnic groups primarily responsible for shaping Bloom's sense of his own identity are the Jewish and the Irish peoples. Other characters' attitudes toward Bloom are conditioned by his Jewishness, which relegates him to a marginal status in a country whose Jews are so small a percentage of the total populace that Mr. Deasy exaggerates only slightly when he claims that the Irish never persecuted the Jews because they "never let them in" (2.437–42/36). In the Cyclops chapter the narrow-minded Citizen challenges Bloom's right to call himself Irish, spitting in disgust when Bloom declares that his "nation" is Ireland (12.1430–33/331), but none of the characters in *Ulysses* question Bloom's status as a Jew. It is ironic, therefore, that in a provocative article whose title encapsulates his thesis, Erwin R. Steinberg has declared that "James Joyce and the Critics Notwithstanding, Leopold Bloom Is Not Jewish." Since Steinberg's analysis raises the important issue of Bloom's ethnic and racial identification, it deserves consideration here.

Steinberg is primarily concerned with arguing, first, that Bloom is not a Jew in the "religious" sense because he neither fits the rabbinical definition of Jewishness nor practices the Jewish religion; and, second, that Bloom is not a "secular" Jew, one who identifies in some broad ethnic or cultural sense with his Jewish heritage without embracing Judaism as a religion. Since Bloom is not circumcised, does not observe kosher dietary laws, never attends synagogue, and makes mistakes when he tries to parade his knowledge of Jewish matters, Steinberg seems generally to be on solid ground in his contention that Bloom is not a "religious" Jew. He stretches the evidence only slightly when he says, "by not a single rite of passage—birth, baptism, circumcision, confirmation, marriage, or planned-for funeral—does Leopold Bloom qualify as being Jewish. In fact, by every one of those rites, he qualifies as a Gentile."[1] Most of this is demonstrably true, the one point of uncertainty being Steinberg's contention that Bloom was not Jewish by birth because his mother, Ellen Higgins, was a Gentile. In support of his position, Steinberg says merely that Bloom's "mother was born a Protestant" (28), but that idea is unsupported by the text of *Ulysses*: in fact, as Shari Benstock has obseved, Ellen Higgins seems to have been a Catholic, since she was buried in a predominantly Catholic cemetery and appears in Circe with an Agnus Dei, crying, "Sacred Heart of Mary, where were you at all at all?" (15.290/438).[2] Yet if Ellen Higgins died a Catholic that does not necessarily mean she was born one, and the chance exists that she was a Jew by birth who later converted to Catholicism. The possibility is enhanced by the fact that while he was writing *Ulysses,* Joyce knew of a family of Dublin Jews named Higgins, and discussed them in 1921 with A. J. Leventhal.[3]

There are, however, various problems in determining ethnic identity through family names, as we might suspect from Stephen Dedalus's "Greek" surname. To begin with, various families in *Ulysses* have changed their names: Bloom's father, Rudolph, changed his name from Virag to Bloom, while Bloom's maternal grandfather, Julius Higgins, was born Julius Karoly (17.534–37/682). Both original family names were Hungarian, although whether Karoly was a Jewish or a Gentile name is unknown. More importantly, as long as Jewish identity is inherited from the mother and the family name is taken from the father, there is no way of determining with absolute certainty whether or not a character was born Jewish without tracing the character's ancestry back to a homogeneous Jewish community. We might assume, for instance, that Ellen Higgins was not Jewish because her mother's maiden name was Fanny Hegarty (17.537/682), yet all we really know is that Fanny had a father named Hegarty—not whether or not *her* mother was Jewish. Conversely, Molly Bloom's mother, "Lunita Laredo," appears to have been a Sephardic Jew (Molly thinks of herself as "jewess looking after my mother" [18.1184–85/771]), but there is always the possibility—unlikely as it seems—that Lunita's mother was a Gentile. If so, then in one sense Molly is a Gentile; if not, she is Jewish, regardless of her belief in the Catholic religion.

Shari Benstock therefore seems quite correct in dismissing "concern . . . with the mother as the transmitter of Jewry" from serious consideration in discussions of *Ulysses*.[4] Steinberg's emphasis on the formal aspects of Judaism is technically correct, but it reaches into an area that is alien to Joyce's more broadly humanistic concept of Bloom's Jewishness. In fact, in Buck Mulligan's "Ballad of Joking Jesus" Joyce seems to satirize this rigid emphasis on a narrowly conceived point of view:

—*I'm the queerest young fellow that ever you heard.*
My mother's a jew, my father's a bird.
With Joseph the joiner I cannot agree.
So here's to disciples and Calvary. (1.584–87/19)

Thus, in one sense, Jesus was a Jew because his mother was Jewish; had he traced his descent from his father, he would have been a bird. Such legalistic definitions come under close scrutiny in *Ulysses* and are always found wanting. For instance, even if we assume that Lunita Laredo was Jewish while Ellen Higgins was a Gentile, we still have to contend with the fact that Molly Bloom does not think of herself as a Jew, while rightly or wrongly, Leopold Bloom thinks he is Jewish. Even more ironically, while Jewish culture traces heritage through the maternal line, Gentiles tend to emphasize the father's background. Thus if Bloom is not Jewish, in the strictly "religious" sense, neither is he a Gentile—or so the Irish Gentiles in *Ulysses* believe; Molly, however, would be accepted as a Gentile because her father was one, and as a Jew because her mother was Jewish. If Molly is less alienated from her society than Bloom often is, perhaps one reason is that she can fit into either the Jewish or the Gentile community, as she chooses, whereas Bloom will never be accepted by the Gentiles and would have to undergo ritual conversion to be fully accepted by the Jews.

If Steinberg is generally on solid factual ground when be discusses

Bloom's relation to "religious" Judiasm, more serious flaws in his argument appear when he contends that Bloom is not a "secular" Jew. Steinberg lists "three precepts widely accepted by secular Jews that function effectively as criteria for defining secular Judaism": 1) "an acceptance of or commitment to being Jewish"; 2) "a commitment to the idea of the Jews as a people"; and 3) "no embracing of a non-Jewish religion" (32). Already there are two minor problems: first, Steinberg never specifies whether one must meet all three criteria to be a secular Jew, or whether fulfilling one or two of these criteria is sufficient; and second, the process of asking secular Jews to define secular Jewry is circular, since one has to be able to identify the secular Jews to know whom to include in the survey.

Even if we accept the definition without question, Steinberg's claim that "Bloom clearly violates all of these criteria" is misleading. Steinberg promises to demonstrate that Bloom "shows no commitment either to being Jewish in any sense or to a common historical future for the Jewish people," but in fact there are several passages in which Bloom certainly apears to accept being Jewish and to affirm his commitment to the Jewish people. Thus, shortly after declaring that he is Irish because he was born in Ireland, Bloom affirms the importance of his Jewish identity as well: "—And I belong to a race too, says Bloom, that is hated and persecuted. Also now. This very moment. This very instant" (12.1467–68/332). It is even harder to overlook Bloom's acceptance of his Jewishness when he jeers at the openly anti-Semitic Citizen, "—Mendelssohn was a jew and Karl Marx and Mercadante and Spinoza. And the Saviour was a jew and his father was a jew. Your God," adding, after Martin Cunningham tells him that Jesus "had no father," "—Well, his uncle was a jew. . . . Your God was a jew. Christ was a jew like me" (12.1804–9/342). Here he not only explicitly identifies himself as a Jew ("Christ was *a jew like me*") and as part of what he believes is a distinguished tradition of Jewish thinkers and composers (although his list is typically Bloomian, containing as it does one non-Jew and three apostates);[5] he also explicitly rejects Christianity, aligning himself with Christ as a Jew but referring to the Christian savior as "*Your* God." Further evidence may be found in the Eumaeus chapter, where Bloom recounts the incident with the Citizen and argues that the Jews played an important and constructive role in the history of Spain and England while "the priest spells poverty" (16.1081–1127/642–44), and in Ithaca, where the narrator describes Bloom's and Stephen's awareness of their different ethnic identities:

> What, reduced to their simplest reciprocal form, were Bloom's thoughts about Stephen's thoughts about Bloom and about Stephen's thoughts about Bloom's thoughts about Stephen?
> He thought that he thought that he was a jew whereas he knew that he knew that he knew that he was not. (17.527–31/682)

Steinberg's assertion that in converting to Catholicism Bloom forsook his Jewish heritage is more plausible than the argument that Bloom never accepts his Jewishness, but even here the issues are far from simple. After all, Bloom apparently never intended to practice the Catholic religion; he became a nominal Catholic in order to marry Molly, and received such skimpy instruction that in Lotus Eaters he thinks he sees the priest shaking drops off the communion wafers and wonders, "are they in water?" (5.346/80)—not realizing that the priest is making the sign of the cross with the wafers. Bloom seems never to have been a practicing Catholic, and it is significant that at Paddy Dignam's funeral Tom Kernan, a former Protestant who "had been converted to the Catholic faith at the time of his marriage" but "had not been in the pale of the Church for twenty years," according to the *Dubliners* story "Grace" (157), instinctively turns to Bloom as the other outsider at a Catholic burial service (6.654–71/105). The point is not that Bloom is a bad Catholic but that he is not a Catholic at all, except in the most technical sense. Aside from his claim to be Irish, he never seriously professes membership in, or allegiance to, any racial, ethnic, national, or religious community except the Jews. Nor do those who know him regard him as anything but a Jew: a passing acquaintance like Ned Lambert might well ask, "—Is he a jew or a gentile or a holy Roman or a swaddler or what the hell is he?"; but those who know him at all know him as a Jew, or, in the more explicit terms of Martin Cunningham, as "a perverted jew . . . from a place in Hungary" (12.1631–35/337). Ironically, Cunningham here describes Bloom's Christian baptism not as a *conversion* (a change from an erroneous to a true religion) but as a *perversion* (a turning to religious error, or apostasy). For Bloom, the truth lies in his Jewish roots.

One further part of Steinberg's case needs examination, since it involves what I believe is a serious misreading of the text. Contending that Joyce "took care to have Bloom deny that he was Jewish" (33), Steinberg cites as evidence the following passage from Eumaeus, in which Bloom describes for Stephen his encounter with the bigoted Citizen at Barney Kiernan's pub: "He called me a jew and in a heated fashion offensively. So I without deviating from plain facts in the least told him his God, I mean Christ, was a jew too and all his family like me though in reality I'm not" (16.1082–85/643). Apparently Steinberg takes "though in reality I'm not" to mean that Bloom is denying that he is a Jew, but this interpretation requires that we ignore Bloom's statement that he did not deviate "from plain facts in the least" when he said, "Christ was a jew like me." More significantly, it overlooks the fact that the passage calls into question the numerous definitions of "Jew." There is the pejorative stereotype, which was what the Citizen meant in calling Bloom a Jew "in a heated manner offensively"; in those terms Bloom is no more a Jew than Christ was. (This is the one definition that fits Reuben J. Dodd, about whom see more below.) Second, there is the definition of a religious Jew, one whose mother was Jewish (like Christ: "*My mother's a jew, my father's a bird*"); in this sense Bloom realizes that he is not a Jew, unlike "Christ . . . and all his family." Finally, there is the broader ethnic sense of the term, and in this way Bloom can identify himself with Christ as a Jew, although immediately he feels compelled to modify his statement to admit that there is also a more technical sense in which he is not really a Jew ("though in reality I'm not").

We might gain more insight into Joyce's treatment of the Jewish theme in *Ulysses* by examining Joyce's explicit attack on anti-Semitism than by focusing on the technicalities of religious Judaism. If Bloom were not a Jew in any other respect, he would still be Jewish in one way: throughout the novel the other characters think of him as a Jew and respond to him in ways that reveal their uneasy awareness of his Jewish identity. In fact, Joyce's presentation of Bloom accords surprisingly well with Jean-Paul Sartre's view that the Jew is the product of Gentile society: that is, that the concept of "Jew" as it exists in the minds of non-Jews is determined by factors that are independent of historical Judaism. Sartre contends that "If the Jew did not exist, the anti-Semite would invent him"; more broadly, "it is the Christians who have *created* the Jew," so that "the Jew is in the situation of a Jew because he lives in the midst of a society that takes him for a Jew."[6] Sartre's comments on the Jewish love of rationality are also illuminating. Bloom's propensity for argument appears ridiculous when the narrator of Cyclops grouses, "I declare to my antimacassar if you took up a straw from the bloody floor and if you said to Bloom: *Look at, Bloom. Do you see that straw? That's a straw.* Declare to my aunt he'd talk about if for an hour so he would and talk steady" (12.893–96 / 316). Yet in the context of the chapter in which Bloom's rational mind is constantly set in motion against the irrationality of the barflies, we might more logically view the situation in Sartre's terms: in argument, he says, "the Jew wishes to destroy . . . the ensemble of irrational values that present themselves to immediate cognition without proof." Moreover, the "perpetual criticism with which [the Jew] is reproached conceals a naive love for a communion in reason with his adversaries, and the still more naive belief that violence is in no way necessary in human relations" (114). Indeed, in the middle of a heated argument in the same chapter Bloom propounds, simplistically but movingly, his "naive belief" in the inefficacy of violence:

> —But it's no use, says he. Force, hatred, history, all that. That's not life for men and women, insult and hatred. And everybody knows that it's the very opposite of that that is really life.
> —What? says Alf.
> —Love, says Bloom. I mean the opposite of hatred. (12.1481–85 / 333)

Bloom, however, is not merely a Jew because others force him into "the situation of a Jew," but because after a great deal of indecision he chooses the role of Jew, asserting his Jewish identity in a forceful and even heroic manner when confronted by the Citizen's anti-Semitic vituperation. We might regard Bloom's development in the novel as the evolution from what Sartre calls the "inauthentic Jew"—one who avoids his Jewishness, preferring assimilation into Gentile culture and the retreat into general concepts of human nature—to the "authentic Jew," who "*makes himself a Jew,* in the face of all and against all." As Sartre notes, such self-assertion is liberating: "At one stroke the Jew, like any authentic man, escapes description" (137). This escape from description or simplistic categorization is not only the mark of Bloom's status as an authentic Jew, but an acknowledgment of his quintessential role as modern man—fully modern, fully human. By contrast, most of the other characters in *Ulysses* are limited: the single culture of the xenophobic Citizen (his counterpart to the single eye of Homer's Polyphemus) is an aspect of his limited vision, while Bloom's dual heritage as Irishman and Jew permits him a broader, stereoscopic vision of the human comedy. Yet Bloom's humanity also rests upon his paradoxical situation: his role as Everyman and Noman (17.2008 / 727), as an Irishman who is not accepted as such, as both Jew and non-Jew. David Daiches, who observes that "Bloom is not a religious Jew," adds perceptively that "It is part of his character as exile that he should not belong fully to *any* community."[7] Bloom's uneasy relationship to his Jewish heritage is thus a crucial aspect of his keylessness, his spiritual wandering between worlds which is our perpetual modern odyssey.

THE CASE OF REUBEN J. DODD

One of the perennial problems facing Joyce's readers is what sorts of "background" information they need to have in order to approach the works, and what uses they might legitimately find for that information. In particular, readers need to be able to distinguish between pieces of information about Joyce's Dublin that may satisfy our curiosity but do not help to elucidate our reading of the text, and those that are clearly helpful, even essential, to our understanding of a work. In the first category I would place the fact that Alfred Hunter, the primary model for Leopold Bloom, was not a Jew.[8] It would be interesting to know whether Joyce was aware that Hunter was a Gentile or whether he shared the misconception about Hunter's background that his brother later passed along to Richard Ellmann,[9] but in neither case would Hunter's status as a Gentile affect Bloom's status as a Jew. On the other hand, precisely the opposite seems to be true in the case of Reuben J. Dodd, the miserly moneylender of *Ulysses* whose real life counterpart, also named Reuben J. Dodd, was an Irish Catholic.

What makes this situation interesting is that a host of important Joyce critics have explicitly or implicitly accepted the fictional Dodd's Jewishness, thereby lending credibility to what is probably the assumption of many novice readers of *Ulysses*: that Dodd is a "bad Jew" introduced for the purpose of contrast with the "good Jew," Bloom. References to Dodd as a Jew seem, however, to have been scarce prior to 1962, when Robert M. Adams criticized Bloom for adopting "the alien [Gentile] point of view with quite unnatural ease, and [taking] the appalling Gentile distinction between 'white Jews' and 'dirty Jews' with all the seriousness of an Englishman." Adams added in a note that "Mr. Ellmann tells me that Reuben J. Dodd was probably not a Jew at all," but he remained convinced that the fictional Dodd is Jewish.[10] Twelve years later Adams still maintained that "In real life, it appears, Reuben J. Dodd was not Jewish, but he is consistently so throughout the novel."[11] Against this mass of popular opinion, however, two scholars have argued that the fictional Dodd is no more Jewish than the historical figure: Father Robert Boyle has contended that Dodd is a Catholic and is probably identified with the character called Harford in the *Dubliners* story "Grace"—a Gentile whose "fellow-travellers" refer to him as "an Irish Jew" because of his stinginess (159); and Louis Hyman has declared flatly that "Dodd, in fact, was an Irish Catholic and not a Jew, as Bloom and all his companions in the funeral cortege knew quite well."[12]

That Dodd is a Jew is, I believe, a misimpression that Joyce wanted to foster in order to make a point about the dangers of racial and religious stereotyping. Ironically, Adams and other readers who regard Dodd as Jewish would logically come to the opposite conclusion: that Joyce himself is guilty, in this instance, of an anti-Semitic bias. Since such a bias would be directly contrary to the humane vision that generally seems to be at the heart of *Ulysses,* we need to examine the possible evidence that might support the idea that Dodd is Jewish. For ease of reference, I have numbered the pieces of evidence that might support such a reading:

1. In Hades, when Dodd is first spotted, Martin Cunningham nudges Mr. Power and says, "Of the tribe of Reuben" (6.251/93), a phrase which on first inspection might seem to refer to one of the twelve tribes of Israel.

2. Dodd is consistently referred to as "blackbearded" and crookbacked (6.252–53/93–94, 10.891/244, 15.1918/497, 15.2145–46/506), which could refer to a stereotyped image of the Jew.

3. Dodd is a usurer, or "gombeen man" (10.890/244), and therefore a member of a profession popularly associated with Jews.

4. Dodd's given name—or, as Joe Hynes would put it, his "christian name" (6.881/111)—sounds Jewish, even if his surname does not.

5. At various times, Dodd is associated with Barabbas (6.274/94, 10.950/245) and Judas Iscariot (11.438–39/267, 15.1918/497); in his final apparition, in Circe, he is transformed into *"Reuben J. Antichrist, wandering jew"* (15.2145/506).

6. After a barroom discussion of a case in which Sir Frederick Falkiner dismissed a suit for arrears of rent brought by Dodd against a poor man, the Citizen seems to refer to Dodd as one of the "strangers" or foreigners who are ruining Ireland (12.1151/323, 12.1156/324).

7. Apparently in reference to the same case, Bloom thinks of Sir Frederick as "The devil on moneylenders. Gave Reuben J. a great

strawcalling. Now he's [Dodd is] really what they call a dirty jew" (8.1158–59 / 183).

Individually, these seven items might not convince us that Dodd is Jewish, but collectively they are far more persuasive. Indeed, if the historical Dodd had not been a Gentile we probably would look no further into the matter. As it is, however, we might do well to reconsider the evidence from a more skeptical point of view:

1. The phrase "of the tribe of Reuben" might be taken not to mean that Cunningham thinks Dodd is literally a Jew but to indicate that he fits the stereotype of the Jewish usurer. If Dodd is the same character as Harford (in "Grace"), as Father Boyle persuasively argues, then Cunningham is merely referring to the popular characterization of Harford or Dodd as the "Irish Jew." (In this context it might be recalled that in "Grace" Cunningham is the character whose "Hm" expresses disapproval of Harford.) Finally, as Adams notes, "The phrase 'of the tribe of Reuben' is customarily applied to Judas Iscariot,"[13] so Cunningham's remark might call attention to Dodd's role as the usurer who betrays his fellow Irishmen when he collects his thirty pieces of silver through interest.

2. Being black bearded and having a crooked back hardly insure that Dodd is Jewish. Note that just after we first see Dodd, we watch Martin Cunningham caress his beard (6.260 / 94), and that in Dodd's last, phantasmogoric appearance in Circe, his crooked back is transferred to Punch Costello (15.2151 / 506), so that his reputedly "Jewish" physical characteristics are shared by Gentile characters.

3. There were Christian usurers in Joyce's Dublin, and only the implicit acceptance of a pejorative stereotype can allow us to assume that a usurer is Jewish until proved otherwise.

4. Although "Reuben" is often a Jewish name, it is not exclusively Jewish. Nor was it unknown for Christians living in late nineteenth- and early twentieth-century Ireland to have Biblical names: *Ulysses* gives us such examples as Adam Findlater (4.128 / 58) and Aaron Figatner (11.149 / 259, 15.4357 / 586) as well as the more prominent Malachi Mulligan and Simon Dedalus, while my own nineteenth-century ancestors included an Irish-American named Lazarus Finney.

5. Identifying Dodd with Jewish characters like Barabbas and Judas Iscariot might be regarded as a way of vilifying him by calling attention to qualities that, in the minds of anti-Semites, are inevitably associated with Jews even though the characters realize that Dodd himself is not really Jewish. The same principle appears to be in operation when Joe Hynes refers to Bridgeman, who lent money to Paddy Dignam, as "Shylock" (12.765/313) even though Bridgeman apparently was a Gentile. The description of Dodd as "*Reuben J. Antichrist, wandering jew*" in Circe might be regarded as the ultimate expression of Dodd's role as the reverse of Bloom: Dodd is symbolically the Antichrist, and Bloom a slightly comic type of Christ, just as Dodd's scant concern for his son, who nearly drowned, is the reverse of Bloom's obsession with his own son, Rudy, who died in infancy.

6. Although a first reading does indeed seem to indicate that the Citizen is referring to Dodd as one of the "strangers" who have invaded Ireland, a second reading reveals that he might equally well be referring to James Wought, the German Jew implicated in the "Canada swindle case" (12.1084/322) which the barflies have just been discussing, since it was the talk of Falkiner's role in that case that led to the story about his dismissal of Dodd's suit.[14] In any event, there is no other evidence that Dodd is foreign born, and we would do well not to place much faith in the ramblings of a xenophobic drunk.

7. Bloom's reference to Dodd as "a dirty jew," taken out of context, might well justify the declaration of various critics that Bloom is indulging in anti-Semitic attitudes here, but if we consider the lack of solid evidence that Dodd is actually Jewish, then we will be inclined to agree with Father Boyle's conclusion that "Bloom is using the language of [the anti-Semites] to condemn, not Jews, but both the Catholic Dodd to whom those other Catholics had applied the opprobrious term and all the other anti-Semites who so readily used it."[15] That is, Bloom recognizes the irony of the anti-Semitic label conventionally applied to Dodd and uses one more to make his own little protest against vicious ethnic stereotyping. This private confrontation with the "dirty Jew" label resurfaces in Eumaeus, when Bloom tells Stephen that the Citizen called him "a jew and in a heated fashion offensively.

So I . . . told him his God, I mean Christ, was a jew too and all his family like me *though in reality I'm not*" (16.1082–85/643; italics added): Bloom's distinction is thus between Dodd, the Catholic who is "*really* what they [the Catholics] call a dirty jew," and Bloom, who "in reality" is not.

Aside from the fact that none of the above arguments in favor of Dodd's Jewishness is convincing, much less conclusive, there are other reasons for supposing that he is a Gentile. First, of course, is the existence of the historical Dodd, a Catholic who sent his son to Belvedere College, where one of his schoolmates was James Joyce. There is no reason why Joyce could not base a Jewish character on a Gentile, of course; he appears to have done so in the case of Bloom and Alfred Hunter. Yet Dodd is different from Hunter-Bloom for two reasons: because Joyce changed Hunter's name but not Dodd's, and because the text specifically identifies Bloom as a Jew (although one with a problematic relationship to his Jewish heritage), whereas Dodd only assumes symbolic Jewish roles (for example, as Judas and the Wandering Jew). Neither of the two pejorative terms commonly applied to Jews in turn-of-the-century Ireland and England, "sheeny" and "jewman," is ever used in connection with Dodd, even though the characters know these terms and are willing to use them in referring to Jews: Mulligan calls Bloom "The sheeny!" and "Ikey Moses" (9.605–7/200–1) and Ben Dollard calls his tailor a "jewman" (10.916/244). Finally, the assumption that Dodd is an Irish Catholic rather than a Jew makes him more obviously the symbolic counterpart to Bloom and allows Joyce to develop his ironic contrast between Bloom, the charitable Jew, and Dodd, the miserly Gentile. Thus when Lenehan says Bloom is off "Defrauding widows and orphans" (12.1622/377)—ironically, just at the time Bloom is trying to help Paddy Dignam's widow and orphans—he instinctively accuses Bloom of the sort of crime Reuben J. Dodd might well commit, simply on account of Bloom's Jewishness; conversely, in referring to Dodd as Judas or Barabbas the characters automatically apply the Jewish label to him on account of his crimes. Thus, to the anti-Semite, if Bloom is a Jew he must be a cheat and a miser, while if Dodd is a cheat and a miser he must be a sort of Jew.

The irony of the situation would have been clearer if Joyce had made it more obvious that Dodd is a Gentile, or if he had included the name of the worker who pulled Reuben, Jr., from the Liffey and received in payment a florin from Reuben, Sr.—"One and eightpence too much," according to Simon Dedalus (6.291/95). In real life, the payment was a half crown and the rescuer was named Moses Goldin, a name that surely justifies Adams's speculation that the rescuer of Dodd, Jr., was in fact Jewish.[16] I suspect that the ideal reading of the entire sequence would involve the initial assumption that Dodd is Jewish and his son's savior a Gentile, followed by the discovery that in fact at least one of these terms is reversed, and that a tacit acceptance of anti-Semitic stereotypes has led us into the trap that Joyce has set for us. This fall into error and ultimate recognition of the source of that error, which resembles the experience of the reader of *Paradise Lost*, as Stanley Fish imagines it in his *Surprised by Sin* (1967), is surely a richer, more satisfying process than it would have been if Joyce had made Dodd more obviously a Gentile; as it is, however, Joyce runs the considerable risk that aside from a handful of Dubliners and scholars with access to the local background of *Ulysses*, most readers will misread the whole sequence to some extent.

For an example of such a misreading, we might turn back to the point in Hades when Cunningham says that they have all applied to Dodd for loans, then modifies his statement—"Well, nearly all of us"—and Bloom begins speaking "with sudden eagerness" about the near-drowning of Dodd's son (6.259 ff./94). Adams tells us that the passage implies "that [Cunningham thinks] Bloom as a Jew is in some sort of complicity with Jewish money-lenders like Dodd," and that Bloom tells the story to disassociate himself from Jews like Dodd.[17] A more plausible reading, based on the assumption that Cunningham and Bloom both know Dodd is a Catholic, is that Bloom is being singled out not as part of a Jewish conspiracy but as someone who is prudent enough to be able to avoid moneylenders altogether. Nobody likes to be identified as the only ant among grasshoppers, however, so Bloom tells the story about Dodd and his son to show that he is really one of the boys, not a stuffed shirt.

ALL TOO IRISH

In the last chapter of *A Portrait of the Artist as a Young Man,* Davin, the self-proclaimed "Irish nationalist," is disturbed and perplexed by Stephen's skeptical attitude toward the revival of Gaelic sports and the budding movement toward Irish political independence. Noting that Stephen has talked both against English literature and against the prevalence of informers in Ireland, Davin asks, "What with your name and your ideas . . . Are you Irish at all?" (202). The question of Irish identity also surfaces frequently in the *Dubliners* stories: in "A Little Cloud," for instance, Thomas Chandler thinks he would have a better chance of being recognized as a poet were his name "more Irish-looking," and in "A Mother," Mrs. Kearney "determined to take advantage of her daughter's name [Kathleen] and brought an Irish teacher to the house." The theme is most prominent in "The Dead," where Gabriel Conroy is badgered by Molly Ivors to make a trip to the West of Ireland and finally, in exasperation, retorts that Irish is not his language and that he is "sick of my own country, sick of it!" (74, 137, 189). In *A Portrait,* the degree of Stephen's Irishness is a concern from the early scene in which Nasty Roche, of all people, calls attention to Stephen's unusual (and un-Irish) name, to the diary entry in which Stephen expresses his fear of an Irish-speaking peasant (9, 251–52). Along with religion, nationality and language are the "nets" that Stephen declares he will escape, and while these terms have a general and abstract meaning, Stephen is thinking primarily of Irish political and cultural nationalism and of the Irish language movement. At the end of the novel, when he writes in his diary that he will "forge in the smithy of my soul the uncreated conscience of my race," Stephen clearly is motivated in part by a desire to remake Irish culture in his own image, to be the creator rather than the product of the Irish national consciousness.

Like Stephen, Joyce set himself apart from the three major movements that challenged British political and cultural hegemony in Ireland. These movements were those involved with Irish political independence, whose last great leader, in Joyce's opinion, was Parnell; the

Gaelic League, which attempted to reintroduce Irish as the country's principal language, along with the Gaelic Athletic Association and other groups involved in the revival of native Gaelic culture; and the Irish Literary Renaissance, whose writers often depended on translations for their knowledge of medieval Irish literature and who intended to create in the English language a uniquely Irish body of literature. All three of these forces make themselves felt in *Ulysses,* but all are subordinated to Joyce's attempt to carry out Stephen's mission by forging an artistic vision of the Irish "conscience," or consciousness, in his novel. If near the end of the novel Stephen can say that "Ireland must be important because it belongs to me" (16.1164–65 / 645), that is because as a figure of the artist he has become responsible for creating the sense of national identity that we see developed in the pages of *Ulysses.*

Among the legends that have shaped the Irish consciousness is the story of the Shan Van Vocht, or Poor Old Woman, who is a traditional figure for Ireland and is associated with the revival of national pride and independence from Britain. The ballad "The Shan Van Vocht," which celebrates the hope, in 1798, that a French invasion of Ireland would liberate the Irish, features the old woman as the voice of liberty, and in Yeats's play *Cathleen Ni Houlihan* (1902) the Old Woman is transformed into "a young girl" with "the walk of a queen" when Irishmen go out to join the French in fighting the British. The opening chapter of *Ulysses* takes place in a Martello Tower which, as Mulligan tells Haines, was built by William Pitt "when the French were on the sea" (1.543– 44 / 17). The line contains an allusion to "The Shan Van Vocht," and it is appropriate that the Poor Old Woman makes an appearance in the chapter as the milkwoman whose lowly position contrasts with the noble hopes expressed in the ballad. Entering what for her would be alien territory—the rent is paid "to the [English] secretary of state for war," Stephen tells Haines (1.540 / 17)—she appears to Stephen as a "wandering crone, lowly form of an immortal serving her conqueror [the Englishman Haines] and her gay betrayer [Mulligan], their common cuckquean" (1.404–5 / 14). Stephen is aware of the old woman's heritage—"Silk of the kine and poor old woman," he thinks, citing two "names given her in old times" (1.403–4/14)—but she isn't, and Haines and Mulligan treat her with condescension.

That the old woman respects the authority of the loud voices of Mulligan and Haines while paying little attention to Stephen suggests that Stephen is at this point a long way from being able to claim that his possession of Ireland confers importance on the country. In fact, shortly thereafter Stephen will tell Haines that he serves "two masters . . . an English and an Italian," to which he adds that there is "a third . . . who wants me for odd jobs" (1.638–41/20). Stephen identifies the English and Italian masters as the British Empire and the Roman Catholic Church but does not specify the nationality or nature of the third; our only clue to the master's identity comes in Stephen's thought of "a crazy queen, old and jealous. Kneel down before me" (1.640/20). The demand that Stephen kneel relates the "crazy queen" to his mother, since Mulligan earlier accused Stephen of failing to accede to his mother's dying request that he kneel down and pray for her. But the "crazy queen" is also Ireland, imagined here as a demented form of the Shan Van Vocht.

It stands to reason that Ireland would be intertwined in Stephen's imagination with his mother, since in *A Portrait of the Artist as a Young Man* Stephen told Davin that Ireland was a devouring mother, "the old sow that eats her farrow" (203). In *A Portrait*, Stephen also thought of the many forces that were attempting to shape him, including the voice of patriotism, which "had bidden him be true to his country and help to raise up her fallen language and tradition" (84). Those voices speak again in *Ulysses*, and the difference between the way in which two of them speak is crucial. The first is the newspaper editor, Myles Crawford, who in the Aeolus chapter asks Stephen to "write something for me. . . . Something with a bite in it." Rather than letters about foot and mouth disease and articles about nationalist meetings—the usual fare of Dublin journalism—Crawford exhorts Stephen to "Put us all into it, damn its soul. Father, Son and Holy Ghost and Jakes M'Carthy" (7.616–22/135). Although Crawford is thinking of a journalistic production, the description suggests the encyclopedic and democratic nature of *Ulysses*, a book in which "Jakes M'Carthy"—the common Dubliner—receives treatment normally accorded to "greater" subjects. The Jakes M'Carthy figures are to be found throughout *Ulysses*, the most important of them appearing under the name Leopold Bloom. In contrast to the Yeatsian emphasis on aristocrats and peasants, with its corresponding distaste for middle-class Dublin, Joyce sets forth as his modern hero an advertising canvasser for whom a prudent concern with finances is not inconsistent with charity and human sympathy.[18] It is Stephen's task, although he does not yet know it, to discover and explore the significance of Jakes M'Carthy, moving from the egotistical and romantic conception of art as self-expression to a broader vision of humanity.

The other voice speaks to Stephen in the Circe chapter, when Stephen encounters a belligerent and drunken British soldier. Although Stephen tries to deflect Private Carr's anger, his witticisms only enrage the soldier, and as the atmosphere becomes more threatening, the prostitutes coalesce into a degraded version of the milkwoman:

> (*The women's heads coalesce. Old Gummy Granny in sugar-loaf hat appears seated on a toadstool, the deathflower of the potato blight on her breast.*)
> STEPHEN
> Aha! I know you, gammer! Hamlet, revenge! The old sow that eats her farrow!
> OLD GUMMY GRANNY
> (*rocking to and fro*) Ireland's sweetheart, the king of Spain's daughter, alanna. Strangers in my house, bad manners to them! (*she keens with banshee woe*) Ochone! Ochone! Silk of the kine! (*she wails*) You met with poor old Ireland and how does she stand? (15.4578–88/595)

Stephen responds "How do I stand you?" although, given his condition, a more immediate problem is how he stands up. In any event, the portrayal of the Shan Van Vocht here is consistently negative: she is a witch seated on a toadstool (compare with 1.401), a reminder of the potato famine, a spirit of revenge like the ghost in *Hamlet*, a wailing woman who, like the Old Woman in *Cathleen Ni Houlihan,* has been set wandering by the many "strangers" in her house. As the farrow-eating sow, she is the worst aspect of Mother Ireland, that which denies to her children any sense of individual identity or of destiny apart from their country's. In "No Second Troy" (1910), Yeats would imagine Maud Gonne as a Helen of Troy turned destructive in an age that lacked heroic stature, but the problem with Old Gummy Granny lies in her parochial narrow-mindedness and her willingness to sponsor violence. Hence it is not long before Joyce describes her handing Stephen a knife and urging him to "Remove him, acushla. At 8.35 a.m. you will be in heaven and Ireland will be free. *(she prays)* O good God, take him!" (15.4737–39/601).

The odd but precise time of Stephen's expected entry into heaven and of Ireland's liberation suggests that Old Gummy Granny is using Dunsink time: the equivalent in Greenwich time, which presumably would be used for official British business, including the execution of Irish martyrs, is 9:00 A.M. The surreal scene enacted here is one way of dramatizing Stephen's fear that Ireland's "freedom" depends on his "death"—the subordination of his own values and desires to those of the community. The implied reference to the dual time scheme, however, reminds us that there is also another viewpoint at hand, and that it belongs to someone who continually tries to see matters from another person's point of view. That someone is Bloom, who will pick Stephen up after Private Carr flattens him.

If Stephen follows Joyce in challenging a preconceived and narrow conception of Irish identity, Bloom embodies the larger perspective toward which Stephen should be working. Continually treated by other characters as an outsider, an alien in his own country, Bloom is an Irishman who fits none of the stereotypes: he is an inept storyteller, an infrequent drinker, a thoughtful and somewhat shy man who is slow to anger and suspicious of ostentatious shows of patriotism. Buck Mulligan, who tells Stephen that they should "work together" to "Hellenise" Ireland, later whispers to Stephen that Bloom is "Greeker than the Greeks" (1.157–58/7, 9.614–15/201), inadvertently hinting at Bloom's Odyssean role; other characters regard Bloom in stereotypically Jewish terms. Bloom does play Irish roles in Circe: he is an Irish entertainer who sings a version of a song that he earlier associated with Corny Kelleher (15.1723–25/491; see 5.12–16/71, 6.686/106). Later he speaks like an Irish peasant in a Synge play: "Let me be going now, woman of the house, for by all the goats in Connemara I'm after having the father and mother of a bating" (15.1962–64/499). Even there, however, Bloom is often an outsider, and his claim to be Irish could be regarded as no less bogus than his many other assumed roles.

While Stephen Dedalus bears the name of an "absurd Greek," Bloom has an equally un-Irish appellation. Had Rudolf Virag, Bloom's father, simply translated the family name from Hungarian when he emigrated to Ireland, he would have emerged with the name Flower, since as Gilbert tells us, *virag* is Hungarian for "flower."[19] What Virag got instead was a name that sounds more Jewish than "Flower," so if the intention was to assimilate into Irish society, the change of names did little to further that end. The point is a relevant one since Bloom is often looked upon as an outsider because his name suggests his family's foreign origins. In the Cyclops chapter, where Irish nationalism is a central theme, it is significant that the Citizen introduces the subject of foreign names—in this case, English names in the lists of births, deaths, and marriages in an Irish paper—almost immediately after the first mention of "the prudent member," our hero, whose own name is Celticized to "O'Bloom, the son of Rory" (12.211–37/297–98). The name O'Bloom does not stick, though, and Bloom—the "bloody freemason," as the Citizen calls him (12.300/300)—finds himself subject to attack as the barflies look for a scapegoat to blame for their problems.

Throughout the chapter, the Citizen assumes that Bloom is somehow not Irish. Alluding to John Kells Ingram's poem "The Memory of the Dead," which celebrates the Irish martyrs who died in the uprising of 1798, the Citizen glares at Bloom, and when he recites "The friends we love are by our side and the foes we hate before us"—from Thomas Moore's "Oh! Where's the Slave, So Lowly"—he is surely thinking of Bloom, with whom he has been arguing, as one of the "foes" whom he hates (12.519–24 / 306). Likewise, when the Citizen begins complaining about foreigners who come to Ireland and swindle the natives, the narrator reports that Bloom "lets on he heard nothing," implying that the complaints were aimed indirectly at Bloom (12.1141–62 / 323–24). Eventually, Bloom enters the political argument, claiming that the root problem is the reliance on force and persecution, and the dialogue leads inevitably to a challenge to Bloom's nationality:

> —Persecution, says he, all the history of the world is full of it. Perpetuating national hatred among nations.
> —But do you know what a nation means? says John Wyse.
> —Yes, says Bloom.
> —What is it? says John Wyse.
> —A nation? says Bloom. A nation is the same people living in the same place.
> —By God, then, says Ned, laughing, if that's so I'm a nation for I'm living in the same place for the past five years.
> So of course everyone had the laugh at Bloom and says he, trying to muck out of it:
> —Or also living in different places.
> —That covers my case, says Joe.
> —What is your nation if I may ask? says the citizen.
> —Ireland, says Bloom. I was born here. Ireland.
> The citizen said nothing only cleared the spit out of his gullet and, gob, he spat a Red bank oyster out of him right in the corner. (12.1417–33 / 331)

Readers of *A Portrait of the Artist* might recall that when Stephen was asked whether he kissed his mother at night, he first answered yes and then no, but both answers resulted in his being ridiculed (14). Stephen assumed that there must be a "right answer" to the question, but Bloom, in similar circumstances, knows that "nation" is a slippery term that requires more than one definition. If political independence is a requirement for nationhood, for example, Ireland in 1904 was not a nation. Even less appropriate are romantic notions of nationality as an expression of racial identity, which of course is what the Citizen is hinting at. As Joyce noted in his 1907 lecture, "Ireland, Island of Saints and Sages," modern civilizations are the result of diverse and intertwined influences, and with rare exceptions such as the Icelanders, no race, especially the Irish, "can boast of being pure today." "Nationality," Joyce continues, may be "a convenient fiction," but if it has any meaning, it "must find its reason for being rooted in something that surpasses and transcends and informs changing things like blood and the human word. . . . Do we not see that in Ireland the Danes, the Firbolgs, the Milesians from Spain, the Norman invaders, and the Anglo-Saxon settlers have united to form a new entity, one might say under the influence of a local deity?" (*Critical Writings* 165–66). And if sharing a single place is what makes a people a nation, as Joyce seems to be saying, and as Bloom initially asserts, then neither the Irish emigrants nor the Jews of the Diaspora form a nation; hence, having referred to "the same people living in the same place," Bloom must immediately open the possibility that a nation consists of people "living in different places."

It would be a mistake, I suspect, to assume that Bloom has any clear and consistent idea of what makes a "nation." In Aeolus, as he watches the newspaper foreman Joseph Patrick Nannetti, he thinks, "Strange he never saw his real country. Ireland my country. Member for College green" (7.87–88/118). Nannetti, he believes, is "more Irish than the Irish" (7.100/119), a phrase that anticipates Mulligan's description of Bloom as "Greeker than the Greeks" and Stephen's dry summation of his father as "all too Irish." Bloom knows that Nannetti "never saw" Italy, apparently because he was born in Ireland, so in thinking of Nannetti as Italian rather than Irish, Bloom defines nationality in the same way that the Citizen will later, at which time Bloom will counter the Citizen's challenge to his Irishness by asserting, "I was born here." Bloom will also contradict his proclamation of Irish nationality when he refers to Shakespeare as "our national poet" (16.782/634, 16.840/636): since Shakespeare was not Irish, Bloom seems to be denying the Irish any national identity apart from the English. Yet to expect Bloom to be consistent in his use of "nation" is surely to ask too much, since the problem, as Bloom realizes, lies precisely with the idea that the word has a single meaning applicable under all circumstances.

One sign of the direct relationship between the Irish and Jewish themes in *Ulysses* is the fact that after proclaiming himself Irish, Bloom immediately turns to his other national or ethnic identification to expound further on the theme of persecution:

> —And I belong to a race too, says Bloom, that is hated and perse-
> cuted. Also now. This very moment. This very instant.
> Gob, he near burnt his fingers with the butt of his old cigar.
> —Robbed, says he. Plundered. Insulted. Persecuted. Taking what
> belongs to us by right. At this very moment, says he, putting up his
> fist, sold by auction in Morocco like slaves or cattle.
> —Are you talking about the new Jerusalem? says the citizen.
> —I'm talking about injustice, says Bloom. (12.1467–74/332)

The fact that both the Irish and the Jews have been victimized by "injustice" is but one of the Irish-Jewish parallels that may be found throughout *Ulysses*. In Aeolus, Professor MacHugh quotes from John F. Taylor's 1901 speech on the importance of the Irish language, a speech that depends upon an extended political and cultural analogy between the Irish under British domination and the Israelites in bond-age in Egypt. Stephen, whom Mulligan styles Wandering Aengus, paral-lels Bloom as the Wandering Jew, and in Ithaca the two exchange "fragments of verse from the ancient Hebrew and ancient Irish lan-guages" (17.724–25/687–88).

Part of Joyce's point is that Ireland's indigenous culture could not sustain it into the twentieth century: the shortest route to Tara may be found in a circuitous journey through Western culture. As Herbert Howarth has pointed out, Taylor's comparison of the Irish and the Israelites was one commonly made during the Irish Literary Renais-sance, and at the same time "the Irish had the sense of an analogy with a Homeric people."[20] While the parallels between the Irish and the Jews, or between medieval Irish and classical Greek literature, were generally set forth to give a respectable pedigree to Irish culture (espe-cially in comparison with the newcomers next door, the English), Joyce established his parallels to undermine ethnic chauvinism and stereotyp-ing. It is for this reason, among others, that he chose Homer's Cyclops as the model for his xenophobic Citizen. All too Irish, despising not only the Jews but all foreign cultures, rejecting all viewpoints except his own, the Citizen is truly a one-eyed man. His limitations are mocked by the chapter's style, which alternates between the rhetorics of inflation and deflation, and by the presence of Bloom, whose dual heritage as Irishman and Jew gives him two cultures (with the unsuspected Greek antecedent adding a third). In this sense, the national or ethnic theme of Joyce's "epic of two races" underscores the book's parallactic vision, providing us with one more example of the limitations inherent in any single perspective on human affairs.

8 ——

Reading in *Ulysses*

In his influential essay, "*Ulysses*, Order and Myth" (1923), T. S. Eliot defended Joyce's novel against charges of formlessness and incomprehensibility by contending that Joyce used a mythological parallel as "a way of controlling, of ordering, of giving a shape and a significance to the immense panorama of futility and anarchy which is contemporary history" (Deming 1:270). Eliot thereby shifted the allegation of chaos and futility from the book to the world, arguing that *Ulysses* made sense even if post-world war European civilization did not. Other reviewers were considerably less charitable: readers were often warned that they would be morally or aesthetically offended by *Ulysses*, or that the book would prove either boring or impenetrable. Holbrook Jackson's review, despite it admission that *Ulysses* "is not indecent," is typical of many reponses in its concern with the problems of Joyce's readers, who are required "to spend a full day" with Leopold Bloom and come to "detest him heartily." Readers, Jackson says, will be affronted by the style, which will make them become "bored, drowsed, bewildered." Even worse is "the arrangement of the book," which omits "the conventions of organised prose which have grown with our race"; from this, Jackson concludes that "Mr. Joyce evidently believes in making it difficult for his readers—but perhaps he wants to scare them away." In any event, "the reader is continually losing his way and having to retrace his steps" (Deming 1:198–200).

The focus on Joyce's readers has not diminished over the years, although in general it has shifted from complaints like Jackson's to considerations of the reading strategies that the book demands. In 1945 Joseph Frank assessed the book's method as one requiring an unusually active reader: according to Frank, "the reader is forced to read *Ulysses* in exactly the same manner as he reads modern poetry—continually fitting fragments together and keeping allusions in mind until, by reflexive reference, he can link them to their complements."[1] Thus the reader becomes Joyce's collaborator in discovering the meaning and order that underlie the book's apparently chaotic shape. During the past decade or two, the influence of reader-oriented criticism has helped to keep attention focused on Joyce's readers. Marilyn French, for instance, has identified the reader of *Ulysses* as the epic hero of the book, adding that "The journey taken in *Ulysses* is the book itself, and only the reader traverses it entirely."[2] Likewise, Brook Thomas has commented perceptively on the role of the reader in *Ulysses*, comparing it to the way Molly Bloom reads books and letters and contending that Leopold Bloom's attempts to educate his wife are analogous to Joyce's efforts on behalf of his ignorant but potentially educable reader.[3]

Although Thomas is certainly correct in associating Molly's reading habits with our own, the character most often seen reading in *Ulysses* is not Molly. Nor is it Stephen Dedalus, despite his impressive array of literary references and his recollection of having read "two pages apiece of seven books every night" during his stay in Paris (3.136/40). More often, our model of the reading experience is Leopold Bloom, who begins his day by reading the partly obliterated text of the legend inside his "Plasto's high grade ha" (4.69–70/56) and continues reading a variety of materials throughout the day and well into the night. It is true that Molly is an avid reader of soft-core pornography (although she objects to *Moll Flanders* because it has a "Molly" in it [18.657–59/756]), but her reading is generally uncritical and lacking in self-consciousness; of the novel genre she might well say what she says about the love letter, that "true or no it fills up your whole day" (18.737–38/758).[4] Bloom, on the other hand, believes that books can improve us in various ways. Thus, while drinking cocoa with Stephen, Bloom "reflected on the pleasures derived from literature of instruction rather than of amusement as he himself had applied to the works of William Shakespeare more than once for the solution of difficult problems in imaginary or real life" (17.384–87/677).

It is unlikely that many readers of *Ulysses* will find it profitable to use Joyce's book precisely as Bloom has used Shakespeare's. Yet we can learn a great deal about ourselves by reading fiction, as Joyce implied when he told Grant Richards that his intention in writing *Dubliners* was to advance "civilisation in Ireland" by giving the Irish people "one good look at themselves in [his] nicely polished looking-glass" (*Letters* 1:64). Indeed, while the title of *Dubliners* is normally taken to be simply a reference to the characters in the stories, identified in terms of the urban environment that entraps them, the book's name might also refer to the people whom Joyce imagined as the primary readers of the collection, the Dubliners who should see their own situations mirrored in the volume's fifteen stories. Those Dubliners might also see reflections of their experience as readers when they watch the characters read, or attempt to read, various texts that focus with suspicious frequency either on death or on escapism.

If *Dubliners* is a "nicely polished looking-glass" wherein we might catch glimpses of ourselves as readers and otherwise, *Ulysses* more closely resembles the "cracked lookingglass" that Stephen holds in his hand in the first chapter (1.146/6). Kenner has called *Ulysses* "a Berlitz classroom between covers," and Wolfgang Iser has commented that the "repertoire of [*Ulysses*] both reflects and reveals the rules that govern its own communication."[5] Watching Bloom read, we see a somewhat distorted version of our own readings, one that makes us more aware of the strategies and assumptions involved in reading. As we proceed, we see how Bloom's reading reflects his situation and his character, and we learn both from his strengths and from his limitations as a reader. If at the end of *Ulysses* we read better than Bloom does, this is partly because we can watch him reading while he cannot watch us.

One of the differences between Molly's reading and Bloom's is that while Molly prefers to regard her reading material as essentially distinct from herself, and to object to books like *Moll Flanders* that appear to blur the line between text and reader, Bloom almost inevitably discovers some relationship between himself and the text at hand. An obvious example is contained in Bloom's reading of the "throwaway" that he receives from a "sombre Y.M.C.A. young man" in the Lestrygonians chapter:

> Heart to heart talks.
> Bloo.... Me? No.
> Blood of the Lamb.
> His slow feet walked him riverward, reading. Are you saved? All are washed in the blood of the lamb. God wants blood victim. Birth, hymen, martyr, war, foundation of a building, sacrifice, kidney burntoffering, druids' altars. Elijah is coming. Dr John Alexander Dowie restorer of the church in Zion is coming.
> Is coming! Is coming!! Is coming!!!
> All heartily welcome. (8.7–16/151)

This passage consists of a single line of narration—"His slow feet walked him riverward, reading"—and several of interior monologue; Bloom's thoughts, in turn, comprise both the text Bloom is reading and his commentary on it. Bloom's momentary assumption that the word beginning "Bloo" is his own name might seem strange to us, but the various texts that he encounters have a habit of referring somehow to him and his situation: earlier in the day, for example, Bloom opened his newspaper directly to an advertisement for Plumtree's Potted Meat (5.144–47/75), a piece of writing that would resonate in his imagination until it would come to seem as if it might well have been written explicitly for him. Similarly, in reading the flyer for Dowie's revival meeting, Bloom is not so far wrong in thinking that it has to do with him: if "Bloo" begins *Blood* rather than *Bloom,* it is still true that the description of the flyer as a "throwaway" connects it to Bloom, and that Bloom's thought of the kidney that he burned that morning is as much a transformation of his own breakfast into religious terms as it is a commentary on the themes of the Dowie flyer.

In Wandering Rocks, Bloom will open the novel *Sweets of Sin* at random and will discover therein a passage that might almost have evolved directly out of his own marital situation. Kenner has noted that Bloom is inadvertently practicing *Sortes Virgilianae* or Virgilian lots, since he begins reading "where his finger opened" (10.607/236).[6] The *Sortes* technique is actually the most common way Bloom reads, at least on 16 June 1904, if we can judge by Bloom's readings of such documents as the newspaper, the throwaway, and *Sweets of Sin*. The procedure and its origins are described in Sidney's *Defense of Poesy:*

> Among the Romans a poet was called *vates,* which is as much as a "diviner," "foreseer," or "prophet," as by his conjoined words *vaticinium* and *vaticinari* is manifest. So heavenly a title did that excellent people bestow upon this heart-ravishing knowledge. And so far were they carried into the admiration thereof that they thought in the chanceable hitting upon any of such verses, great fore-tokens of their following fortunes were placed. Whereupon grew the word of Virgilian lots, when by sudden opening [of *The Aeneid*] they lighted upon some verse of his (as is reported by many), whereof the histories of the Emperors' lives are full.[7]

The tradition Sidney is describing dates back at least to the first century after Virgil's death. Later, Saint Augustine reported being told by a child's voice to take up a Bible and read; the book fell open to Romans 13:13, an attack on lust that Augustine read as a providential allusion to his own sinfulness. Petrarch, in turn, randomly opened Augustine's *Confessions* during his ascent of Mont Ventoux and discovered that it seemed to refer directly to his own situation. Similar occurrences may be found in English literature: in *Robinson Crusoe,* for example, where a chance opening of the Bible to Psalms 50 contributes to Crusoe's repentance; in Tennyson's "Enoch Arden," where Annie uses the technique to find whether or not Enoch is dead (but misinterprets the text, assuming that "Under the palm-tree" is a metaphor for heaven rather than a literal description of her husband's location); and in Malcolm Lowry's *Under the Volcano,* whose protagonist, Geoffrey Firmin, practices what he calls "sortes Shakespeareanae."

In these acts of reading and interpretation, then, Bloom is taking part in a tradition with a respectable pedigree, albeit one at odds with his generally scientific and rational approach to life. It is interesting that when he looks randomly at a text he finds some personal significance, but when he tries to regularize the process, he has less success. Thus the voice that catechizes itself in the Ithaca chapter reports that Bloom has had only qualified success in solving problems by consulting Shakespeare: "In spite of careful and repeated reading of certain classical passages, aided by a glossary, he had derived imperfect conviction from the text, the answers not bearing in all points" (17.389–91 / 677). Readers of *Ulysses* (and, even more, of *Finnegans Wake*) know pretty much how Bloom felt.

Bloom's inability to discover clear and certain meanings in Shakespeare suggests one of his many connections with Stephen, who develops an elaborate theory about *Hamlet,* but when asked "Do you believe your own theory?" immediately answers "No" (9.1065–67 / 213–14). Stephen develops his theory not merely as a demonstration that *Hamlet* is based on Shakespeare's alleged cuckolding, but as an attempt to define his own relation to the play; his statement that he does not believe his theory is both a refusal to expand this personal interpretation to the realm of objective fact and an admission that any reading based on selected passages is bound to be found lacking, "the answers not bearing in all points." Even so, Stephen is correct in asserting that all readings—of the book and the world—are inevitably personal readings: "We walk through ourselves, meeting robbers, ghosts, giants, old men, young men, wives, widows, brothers-in-love, but always meeting ourselves" (9.1044–46 / 213). This process through which we discover ourselves (imperfectly) in a book is neatly reversed in the Circe chapter, when Stephen and Bloom look into a mirror and see *"the face of William Shakespeare, beardless . . . rigid in facial paralysis, crowned by the reflection of the reindeer antlered hatrack in the hall"* (15.3821–24 / 567). Note that if Bloom's readings of, and reflections on, Shakespeare produce imperfect answers, the literal reflection of Stephen and Bloom produces an imperfect Shakespeare, for every creative act involves an element of distortion just as every act of interpretation is, in the terminology of another Bloom, a "misreading."

We have a good example of Leopold Bloom's misreading fairly early in *Ulysses,* when Molly asks him to interpret a puzzling passage in the book she has just read: *Ruby: the Pride of the Ring.* Molly's problem involves a word that (as we discover later—8.112/154) she pronounces "met him pike hoses." The original passage is important enough to quote at length:

—Met him what? he asked.
—Here, she said. What does that mean?
     He leaned downward and read near her polished thumbnail.
—Metempsychosis?
—Yes. Who's he when he's at home?
—Metempsychosis, he said, frowning. It's Greek: from the Greek. That means the transmigration of souls.
—O, rocks! she said. Tell us in plain words.
     He smiled, glancing askance at her mocking eyes. The same young eyes. The first night after the charades. Dolphin's Barn. He turned over the smudged pages. *Ruby: the Pride of the Ring.* Hello. Illustration. Fierce Italian with carriagewhip. Must be Ruby pride of the on the floor naked. Sheet kindly lent. *The monster Maffei desisted and flung his victim from him with an oath.* Cruelty behind it all. Doped animals. Trapeze at Hengler's. Had to look the other way. Mob gaping. Break your neck and we'll break our sides. Families of them. Bone them young so they metamspychosis. That we live after death. Our souls. That a man's soul after he dies, Dignam's soul. . . .
—Did you finish it? he asked.
—Yes, she said. There's nothing smutty in it. Is she in love with the first fellow all the time?
—Never read it. Do you want another?
—Yes. Get another of Paul de Kock's. Nice name he has.
     She poured more tea into her cup, watching it flow sideways.
     Must get that Capel street library book renewed or they'll write to Kearney, my guarantor. Reincarnation: that's the word. (4.336–61/64–65)

Throughout this passage two sorts of things are going on. First, and more obviously, we are being introduced to, or reminded of, major themes of the book. Metempsychosis is not only a word that occurs in Molly's book (and, appropriately enough, a word "from the Greek") but a major theme in *Ulysses* where Bloom is, in Kenner's terms, a "wily wandering Greek [hero] . . . reincarnated as a wandering home-body Jew."[8] This theme of reincarnation, return, or renewal generally, spills over into Bloom's thoughts, which is probably why he unexpectedly thinks of a library book whose loan needs to be renewed. The idea of renewal is also implied in the way the passage returns us to motifs that have been introduced earlier in the book. For example, we are reminded of Bloom's interest in cruelty, an interest evident earlier in the morning in Bloom's thoughts about his cat: "Cruel. Her nature. Curious mice never squeal. Seem to like it" (4.27–28 / 55). The sadomasochistic theme reappears in Bloom's thoughts about the servant girl next door, so that by the time we watch Bloom reading *Ruby* we are prepared for his interest in the "fierce Italian with carriagewhip" standing over the naked girl; the connection between violence and comedy ("Break your neck and we'll break our sides") is more unexpected but no less perceptive an observation.

Our introduction to such themes as metempsychosis and sadomasochism so dominates this passage that it risks overshadowing the second, related, job of the passage, which is to demonstrate how Bloom reads. Bloom's reading is filled with personal associations that he believes help him to understand the text, as when he thinks of the difference between the way he responded to the trapeze artists at Hengler's circus (by looking away) and the way the rest of the crowd responded (by gaping). Until just a few years ago, it was possible to believe that Bloom was doing a good job of impromptu criticism of *Ruby*, but Mary Power's discovery of Amye Reade's *Ruby. A Novel. Founded on the Life of a Circus Girl* (1889) introduces a new element in the equation.[9] Power demonstrates conclusively that Joyce modeled *Ruby: the Pride of the Ring* after *Ruby. A Novel*, but she also notes that there are significant differences between Amye Reade's *Ruby* (1) and the version in *Ulysses* (*Ruby* 2): in addition to changing the subtitle, Joyce alters the name of Signor Enrico to Signor Maffei and adds a key word that does not appear in *Ruby* 1: metempsychosis. All of these changes are made by Joyce, not by Bloom, and only a knowledge of the original *Ruby* allows us to enjoy the ironies of *Ruby* 2: the subtitle "Pride of the Ring," for instance, is ambiguous unless we know that the book is about a circus, while "metempsychosis" introduces an element that, as Power says (121), is relevant to *Ruby* 1 (where it does not appear) but is even more important to *Ulysses*, a book in which it appears solely on the authority of Joyce's emendation of *Ruby*. Note that the word also appears in *Ulysses* directly as a result of Molly Bloom's faith in her husband's powers of interpretation, her respect for his vocabulary and for his knowledge of literature.

Joyce's change of Enrico (Henry) to Maffei is equally significant, for it shifts the text of *Ruby* 2 away from what would be a natural tendency to identify Signor Enrico with Leopold Bloom, alias Henry Flower.[10] The abandonment of Enrico therefore lets Bloom off the hook and allows him to think disparagingly of other people's cruelty. It is interesting that the sentence that Bloom reads appears almost exactly as in *Ruby* 1, except that the name Maffei has been added: there would have been no direct reference to Henry if the sentence had been printed without alteration, but as soon as a diligent scholar like Mary Power located the original *Ruby*, it would have appeared that the passage referred obliquely to Bloom, that he was in effect reading about himself and censoring a text that associated him with cruelty. The way similar names seem to imply guilt by association is indicated not only in Molly's dislike of *Moll Flanders* but also in the fact that whenever Bloom thinks about the Phoenix Park murders case he is either wrong (5.378–82/81, 16.1053–54/642) or uncertain (8.442–43/163) about the first name of the informer, James Carey, possibly because James Joyce wants to avoid any personal association with an informer.

We can't call "Maffei" a misreading on Bloom's part, but it is a sort of collaborative error by Joyce and Bloom, and (until the discovery of Amye Reade's original *Ruby*) a private joke of the author, to boot. Bloom makes a real error—one that remained undiscovered until

Power published her find—when he thinks, "Must be Ruby pride of the on the floor naked": actually, according to Power, Bloom is looking at the picture of another woman, Victoria Melton. This is the sort of erroneous snap judgment that we all make, one comparable to the assumption made by one of my undergraduate students that *Surprised by Sin* is a pornographic novel while *Venus in Furs,* which happened to be on the same shelf, is about classical mythology. Likewise, some readers who learn that Bloom has made a mistaken identification of the woman in the picture may well remember that when they first read *Ulysses* they initially assumed, as the real John Eglinton admitted that he did, that the Ulysses of the title was Stephen Dedalus (Deming 2:578). Having mistaken Victoria Melton for Ruby, Bloom will misidentify another woman later, when he speculates that the woman he sees with George Russell "might be Lizzie Twigg" (8.527/165); as Zack Bowen has shown, it is more likely that Bloom is looking at Susan Mitchell.[11]

In a letter to Harriet Shaw Weaver, Joyce said that Ezra Pound "understood certain aspects of [*Ulysses*] very quickly" and made "brilliant discoveries and howling blunders" (*Letters* 1:249). On a lower level, most of us read erratically, like Pound, just as on a still lower level Bloom proves an adequate interpreter of *Ruby* (a book, let it be remembered, that he has not read) but manages to damage his own credibility—with us, not with Molly—by making a howling blunder when he tries to clarify his definition of metempsychosis. Immediately after thinking of the word he has been searching for— *reincarnation*—he gives Molly a lucid definition of the term, then muddies the waters by giving an example inspired by the *Bath of the Nymph* picture hanging over the bed: "—Metempsychosis, he said, is what the ancient Greeks called it. They used to believe you could be changed into an animal or a tree, for instance. What they called nymphs, for example" (4.375–77/65). Bloom has tried to define metempsychosis but instead has given an example of metamorphosis. Ironically, this erroneous example developed out of Bloom's ruminations on "Naked nymphs: Greece: and for instance all the people that lived then" (4.372–73/65), thoughts that are relevant to our reading of *Ulysses* because they not only remind us of Bloom's sexual interests and of the book's ubiquitous Hellenic theme, but metempsychotically connect the world of *Ulysses* to ancient Greece and "all the people that lived then." Bloom's error, which he repeats in Nausicaa (13.1118–19/377), is significant in another way, too, for metamorphosis is a theme already associated with Stephen Dedalus, both through the Ovidian reference in his surname and through his musings on supernatural metamorphosis (the Holy Ghost changing into a bird to impregnate Mary) and protean shape-changing. It is only upon rereading that we are likely to discover these parallels, however, at which time Bloom's errors become our portals of discovery.

Elsewhere in Calypso, Bloom takes extended looks at two other texts: Milly's letter and the *Titbits* story, "Matcham's Masterstroke." Milly's letter (4.397–414/66) sets up a number of significant motifs, including the salutation "Dearest Papli," the phrase "beef to the heels," and the song "Seaside Girls." Aside from this thematic importance, the letter allows us another glimpse at the reading process, which begins a few pages earlier with Bloom's skimming of the letter ("Thanks: new tam: Mr Coghlan: lough Owel picnic: young student: Blazes Boylan's seaside girls"—4.281–82/62),[12] continues with the text of this chatty and occasionally ungrammatical letter, and concludes with Bloom's interpretation of the postscript—"Excuse bad writing. Hurry. Piano downstairs. Coming out of her shell" (4.421–22/66). The postscript itself says merely "Excuse bad writing am in hurry. Byby," but Bloom is surely correct in associating Milly's rush to finish writing the letter with the presence of the picnickers congregated downstairs at the piano, and to interpret the letter generally as meaning that Milly is "coming out of her shell." This is a simple text to work on, one for which Bloom's powers of interpretation are sufficient.

In the case of the prize *Titbits* story by Philip Beaufoy, Bloom needs hardly any interpretive ability at all, only the good sense to be able to judge a work like "Matcham's Masterstroke," which he reads while seated in the outhouse:

It did not move or touch him but it was something quick and neat.
Print anything now. Silly season. He read on, seated above his own
rising smell. Neat certainly. *Matcham often thinks of the masterstroke by which he won the laughing witch who now.* Begins and
ends morally. *Hand in hand.* Smart. He glanced back through what
he had read and, while feeling his water flow quietly, he envied
kindly Mr Beaufoy who had written it and received payment of
three pounds, thirteen and six. (4.511–17/69)

Bloom has sized up Beaufoy's work as a formula story, executed com-
petently (unlike Bloom's bowel movement, it is "quick and neat"),
ending not only morally but positively (*"hand in hand"*), but basically
trite ("Print anything now. Silly season"): the sort of story, that is, that
you would read in the jakes, or in the dentist's office, rather than in the
library. In almost every sense, "Matcham's Masterstroke" is the literary antithesis of *Ulysses:* Beaufoy's brief story begins conventionally
and ends happily, Joyce's long novel begins somewhat unconvention-
ally and ends ambiguously; the story Bloom reads is "neat certainly"
and makes few demands on its reader (who picked it up precisely
because it was "something new and easy"—4.501/68), while the
book we are reading is, in Holbrook Jackson's memorable phrase, "an
ungainly, loose-limbed book which falls to pieces as you read it"
(Deming 1:199) and at times requires a serious effort on the reader's
part just to follow the narrative line. H. G. Wells complained, in his
review of *Portrait,* that "Mr. Joyce has a cloacal obsession. He would
bring back into the general picture of life aspects which modern drain-
age and modern decorum have taken out of ordinary intercourse and
conversation" (Deming 1:86); yet while *Ulysses* includes scenes that
are too strong for H.G. Wells (or, I suppose, Philip Beaufoy), it contains little, if anything, that is predictable and false. Bloom's final use
of Beaufoy's story—as toilet paper (4.537/70)—might well be regarded as an appropriate act of literary criticism; hence, in Circe,
when Beaufoy appears to accuse Bloom of plagiarizing and disfiguring
his work, Bloom answers the charges by describing the story as "bad
art" (15.814–40/458–59).[13] Likewise, Bloom proves an able critic of

political rhetoric at the end of the Sirens chapter, when he farts while reading Robert Emmet's last words (11.1284–94 / 291).

For Bloom, a practical man, reading is generally a means to an end, whether that end be instruction (as in the case of Shakespeare's works), sexual arousal (as with *Sweets of Sin*), or something else. The use of the *Titbits* page as toilet paper indicates another aspect of Bloom's use of reading materials: their employment as physical objects independent of whatever writing they might contain. Stephen does something similar, of course, when he tears off part of Mr. Deasy's letter to write his poem; the connection is even reinforced, inadvertently, by Myles Crawford's comment on the torn letter: "Who tore it? Was he short taken?" (7.521 / 132). Yet Stephen's action is a more traditionally artistic one, akin to that of the medieval scribe who decides to write his own poem in the margin of some less interesting document, or the artist who uses another painting as his canvas. Bloom, on the other hand, seems always to be aware of the way the physical existence of the printed or handwritten page opens it up to nonliterary uses. Some of these uses prove failures, as when Bloom throws the crumpled Dowie flyer into the Liffey in an attempt to outwit the seagulls; others carry unacceptable risks, as Bloom reflects in Ithaca when he thinks about "the insecurity of hiding any secret document behind, beneath or between the pages of a book" (17.1413–14 / 709).

A look at the uses to which Bloom puts the flyer for Agendath Netaim illustrates the tendency of reading materials to serve both literary and extraliterary functions, simultaneously existing as collections of words or ideas that impress themselves on the mind and as physical items. Indeed, within the narrative proper, the announcement first serves as wrapping paper in a butcher's shop; Bloom, who picks up the notice to read it, finds a single sheet sufficient, while Dlugacz picks up two sheets to wrap sausages, one sheet being insufficient to prevent leakage. Later, Bloom will find two other uses for the flyer: at the end of Lestrygonians he takes it out of his pocket and pretends to read it so as to appear not to notice Boylan, and in Ithaca he takes it out again and burns it. Even when Bloom actually reads the notice, the narration often refers in some way to its physical existence, the one aspect of any text that clearly separates it from other texts. Note, for example, the description of Bloom's first encounter with the flyer:

> He took a page up from the pile of cut sheets: the model farm at Kinnereth on the lakeshore of Tiberias. Can become ideal winter sanatorium. Moses Montefiore. I thought he was. Farmhouse, wall round it, blurred cattle cropping. He held the page from him: interesting: read it nearer, the title, the blurred cropping cattle, the page rustling. A young white heifer. . . . He held the page aslant patiently, bending his senses and his will, his soft subject gaze at rest. The crooked skirt swinging, whack by whack by whack. (4.154–64/59)

Although the physical existence of the notice, which establishes its spatial dimensions, apparently distinguishes it from the world around it, Bloom's reading blurs that distinction until it can be said of the Agendath Netaim flyer, as Colin MacCabe has said of *Ulysses*, that "it is impossible to isolate the words of the text from the contemporary words surrounding it: the words of the reader. Despite appearances there is no definite limit to a book."[14] Moreover, Bloom's reference to the "young white heifer" seems to describe the "nextdoor girl" rather than one of the blurred cattle in the picture, so that the text Bloom is reading and the one in which he exists form a continuum. The simultaneous emphasis on the physical separateness of the text and on its linguistic continuity with, or dependency on, the larger text, relates virtually all of Bloom's reading materials to *Ulysses* itself, that is, to a book that focuses our attention both on its existence as a physical object, a product of print technology, and on its relationship to the literary, historical, economic, political, and biographical contexts in which it was conceived, written, and printed.

Bloom's tendency to internalize the texts he reads, and thereby to appropriate them for his own uses, is related to his treatment of texts as objects or possessions and reinforced by the fact that, as a typically modern reader, he reads silently. Silent reading, as George Steiner has noted, is a "late historical development," the by-product of a bourgeois civilization that values privacy and individuality.[15] Likewise, Walter Ong has written that "Oral communication unites people in groups. Writing and reading are solitary activities that throw the psyche back on itself." Moreover, according to Ong, "The advent of print intensified the inwardness fostered by script. The age of print was immediately marked in Protestant circles by advocacy of private, individual interpretation of the Bible, and in Catholic circles was marked by the growth of frequent private confession of sins, and concomitantly a stress on the examination of conscience."[16] For a highly literate man like Leopold Bloom—a man whose early literary efforts involved anagrams on his name and a poem with an "acrostic upon the abbreviation of his first name" (17.404–16 / 678) and who now makes his living through printed advertisements—written or printed language is something that you experience silently, and therefore alone.

Bloom is not the only silent reader in *Ulysses,* but the other examples are generally people who are also isolated in some way. I have called attention elsewhere[17] to the way Stephen Dedalus reads silently, both in *A Portrait of the Artist as a Young Man* and in *Ulysses,* so I won't repeat that case here. Instead, I would like to call attention to Master Patrick Dignam, who stops in front of "the window of Madame Doyle, courtdress milliner" to read the announcement of the Keough-Bennett prize fight while two mirrors in the window reflect his image. Master Dignam resembles Stephen and Bloom in being a solitary figure dressed in mourning; he is also one of the rare minor characters whose interior monologues are presented for our inspection. That interior monologue combines with the text of the announcement in Master Dignam's silent reading: "From the sidemirrors two mourning Masters Dignam gaped silently. Myler Keough, Dublin's pet lamb, will meet sergeantmajor Bennett, the Portobello bruiser, for a purse of fifty sovereigns. Gob, that'd be a good pucking match to see. Myler Keough, that's the chap sparring out to him with the green sash. Two bar entrance, soldiers half price. I could easy do a bunk on ma. Master Dignam on his left turned as he turned. That's me in mourning" (10.1132–38).

Master Dignam is less literate than Bloom, less accustomed to skimming texts for their essence; thus he reads whole sentences or phrases from the poster without seeming to transform them in any way. Nonetheless the act of reading calls upon his powers of interpretation (he decides, on the basis of a green sash, which of the pictured boxers is Irish); it raises a practical consideration (how can he get the money for the fight from his mother?); and it results in a moment of self-awareness as he sees himself in a mirror. Later in the scene, the boy will think of other people reading his father's obituary in the evening newspaper—an obituary that we will eventually see Leopold Bloom read, complete with various printer's errors including the abbreviation of his name to "*L. Boom*" (16.1260/647).

That Master Dignam, Stephen, and Bloom (or Boom) read differently from most other characters in the book would be easy to demonstrate. Virtually everyone else reads aloud: Bantam Lyons cannot even skim the racing news without murmuring "Ascot. Gold cup. . . . Half a mo. Maximum the second" (5.532–33/85). Other readings take on the aura of public performances—for example, when the Citizen reads the *Irish Independent*'s list of recent births, deaths, and marriages, emphasizing the large number of non-Irish names (12.219–237/298). The purely verbal quality of these oral readings contrasts with the tendency of Bloom's readings to focus on the visual aspects of a piece—on the inappropriateness of placing an ad for Plumtree's Potted Meat "under the obituary notices" (8.744/171), for example, or the "crooked botched print" in a copy of Aristotle's *Masterpiece* (10.586/235). When Bloom reads his letter from Martha Clifford, he notes two typographical errors; when he reads the Dignam obituary, he discovers various printer's errors as well as errors of fact concerning attendance at the funeral. Bloom's professional immersion in, and awareness of, print helps to force his attention on these visual elements of the text. His commercial interests are related to print culture in another way, for print is associated with a double sense of literary proprietorship: the individual reader is the owner of the physical book itself, while the author is the owner of the words contained therein. (Thus Ong notes that the concept of plagiarism does not exist in purely oral cultures, where private ownership of a linguistic event would seem to be at odds with the communal nature of oral performance.)[18]

The confusion over ownership of a book—whose book is it, the author's or the reader's?—is one aspect of the fundamental duality of the author (or reader) and his other self. In practice, the author imagines a reader who, like Baudelaire's *hypocrite lecteur,* is his double, his brother; likewise, the reader creates the author in his own image. The early scene in which Bloom envies "kindly Mr Beaufoy" is a good example of the reader creating an author who reflects himself, while Beaufoy's charge of plagiarism in Circe (15.822/458) suggests Bloom's uneasy awareness that authors also exist not merely as extensions of ourselves but as distinct individuals whose rights do not end when we purchase their stories.

The connections between reader and writer are crucial to my own understanding of *Ulysses.* Fritz Senn has described the reading of *Ulysses* as an activity requiring continual "righting" of the text. "Readers," according to Senn, "are mediators who shape, or forge, the matter at hand"—people, that is, who are much like authors in their righting / wrighting / writing of the text.[19] Joyce implies the connection in another way at the end of the *Portrait,* in Stephen's diary, where the historical author and the present reader are merged in the figure of Stephen Dedalus, whose silent composition and perusal of his text places him on both sides of the literary confessional. The feat is repeated in *Ulysses,* with a twist, in the scene where Bloom silently writes (and reads) a letter to Martha Clifford, using the pseudonym Henry Flower and disguising his handwriting, but murmurs aloud bits and pieces from an entirely different letter—one he is *not* writing—to conceal his activity from Richie Goulding. Vocal reading is normally a sign of community, a shared experience, and it is a mark of Bloom's isolation from his environment that this rare example of his vocal reading is a carefully constructed fiction. In his silent composition and perusal of the real letter, and indeed in his largely silent meditations throughout the novel, Bloom is both author and reader; in his murmuring of a phony letter whose text exists nowhere but in his own breath, Bloom is not so much author or reader as a character in a fiction of his own creation.

I began this chapter with a reference to the mirroring effects of literature, and it is to this idea that I want to return in my conclusion. The mirror, of course, is one of the most common metaphors for art, but it seems to me peculiarly appropriate in relation to the experience of the reader. In a work of literature, presumably, we "see ourselves," which suggests one parallel with the act of looking in a mirror; moreover, while Buck Mulligan speaks to his image in the mirror in Telemachus (1.121/6)—a feat repeated by Issy in *Finnegans Wake*—looking into a mirror is normally a silent activity, comparable in that respect to the way most of us read. Finally, mirroring always involves some distortion or disorientation; extreme examples may be found in the concave and convex mirrors in Circe that produce variant Blooms (15.145–49/433–34), but even the most perfect mirror reverses left and right. Reading words in a mirror, then, is not an activity that we can perform by simple habit, passively. To read a mirrored text—as Bloom must do in reversing the letters on the titles of the books that he sees in his mirror (17.1357–1414/708–9)—we must read actively, actually creating a new mental perspective for ourselves as we go along.

This, I think, is what Joyce demands that we do, and what he shows us occurring in Bloom's readings, both of the book and of the world. Bloom questions himself, backtracks, tries another perspective, judges the logic of whatever he reads. Whereas Homer's Odysseus was the product of an oral culture, one in which all literary values are inevitably communal values, Bloom stands in the midst of the individualistic, modern age: created by a self-exiled author whose persona in an earlier novel had spoken of "forging" a national "conscience" or consciousness—not reflecting or even reviving it, but creating it— Bloom is likewise a loner who internalizes his world, transforms it, judges it. In this transformation, he reflects our own experience as readers of our texts, interpreters of an age in which we continually feel displaced and seek comfort not in traditional knowledge but in our own resources as "competent keyless citizen[s]" (17.1019/697). If the logic of the Homeric analogy suggests a metempsychotic connection between Odysseus and Leopold Bloom, the logic of the book's representation of reading should give us, as readers, a shock of recognition every time we watch Bloom reading part of the book that we are reading. If this is a further example of metempsychosis, of Bloom somehow being reincarnated in us, so be it.

Appendix:
An Outline of *Ulysses*

Ulysses is divided into three numbered sections that Joyce designated the Telemachiad, the Odyssey (or Wanderings), and the Nostos (Return), paralleling the narrative structure of the *Odyssey*. These sections are in turn divided into a total of eighteen unnumbered chapters—three each in the Telemachiad and Nostos, twelve in the Odyssey—that Joyce referred to by titles derived from characters and events in the *Odyssey*. Although Joyce used these Homeric episode titles in his notes and correspondence, and in the *Little Review* serialization of the first fourteen chapters, he omitted them from the published text; even after book publication, however, he continued to refer to chapters by their Homeric titles, and he encouraged such commentators as Stuart Gilbert and Frank Budgen to use the titles. In this book I have followed the common practice of using the Homeric titles, both as a matter of convenience and as a means of recognizing their place in the composition and critical history of *Ulysses*.

All of the events of *Ulysses* take place in or near Dublin on Thursday, 16 June 1904, and the early morning hours of 17 June. The synopsis that follows is intended only as a bare-bones summary for beginning readers.

CHAPTER 1: TELEMACHUS

Ulysses opens at the Martello Tower in Sandycove, south of Dublin, where Stephen Dedalus has been living with Malachi ("Buck") Mulligan—a medical student—and an Englishman named Haines, who has come to study Celtic literature and culture. Stephen feels alienated from the flippant Mulligan and the condescending Haines, and his dissatisfaction increases when an old milkwoman, whom he regards as a symbol of Ireland, pays greater respect to them than to him. At the end of the chapter Mulligan takes a swim while Stephen, silently vowing not to return home that night, leaves for his teaching job at a private school in Dalkey.

In the Homeric analogy, Stephen is comparable to Telemachus, who sets out to look for news of his father, Odysseus, who has not returned home in the decade following the end of the Trojan War. Since Stephen is not in fact looking for his father, the analogy has nothing to do with his conscious intentions. It refers primarily to his eventual meeting with Leopold Bloom, his symbolic father, as well as to his musings, in later chapters, on the relationship between fatherhood and artistic creation. In this section, Haines and Mulligan play the part of Penelope's suitors, who have taken over Odysseus' palace.

CHAPTER 2: NESTOR

The chapter begins with Stephen trying, with little success, to handle a history class at Mr. Deasy's private school, where he has been teaching for a few weeks. After class, Stephen collects his salary from Mr. Deasy, who asks Stephen to try to place his letter on hoof and mouth disease with the editor of a newspaper. Mr. Deasy also offers Stephen advise on money, women, Irish history, and the Jews who, he claims, are controlling England.

In the *Odyssey,* Nestor is the wise and hospitable (but somewhat garrulous) king of Pylos, whom Telemachus visits in book 3. Joyce's Nestor, Mr. Deasy, is far from wise or charitable: he is a misogynist and anti-Semite whose prejudices stand in stark contrast to the open-mindedness that Joyce will portray in Bloom.

CHAPTER 3: PROTEUS

Since Thursday is a half day at the school, Stephen has the rest of the day off. He walks along the beach at Sandymount Strand, toward Dublin, musing on a variety of subjects that range from the Arian heresy to his months living in Paris. Much of the chapter deals with the processes of transformation, a natural subject for a scene set on the margin between land and sea.

In the fourth book of the *Odyssey,* Telemachus goes to see Menelaus, king of Sparta, to ask if he knows where Odysseus is. Menelaus had learned from Proteus, the shape-changing Old Man of the Sea, that Odysseus is being held captive on an island by Calypso, a sea nymph. The search for directions comes into play in this chapter of *Ulysses,* as Stephen considers whether or not to pay a visit to his maternal uncle, Richie Goulding (he decides against it), but the primary analogy may be between Stephen's vocation as an artist—a transformer of reality—and his thoughts about the way matter is transformed through recurrent natural cycles.

CHAPTER 4: CALYPSO

This episode begins Part II of *Ulysses,* the odyssey of Leopold Bloom. Bloom goes to a pork butcher's shop to buy a kidney, returns home to make breakfast for his wife, Molly, and reads a letter from Milly, his daughter, who is working in a photography shop in Mullingar. He learns that Molly will be visited by Hugh ("Blazes") Boylan, a concert promoter, later that day. Molly's encounter with Boylan will be on Bloom's mind for much of the day, for Bloom suspects (correctly, as we discover) that Molly will have an affair with Boylan. The chapter concludes with Bloom setting forth for the day's adventures from his home at 7 Eccles Street.

Calypso's island is the place where we finally meet Odysseus in the *Odyssey*. In Homer's poem, Odysseus completes the round-trip home that began when he set forth from Ithaca for the Trojan War; Telemachus, however, sets forth from Ithaca to seek news of his father, and returns there in time to meet Odysseus at the hut of the swineherd Eumaeus. In *Ulysses*, however, the reverse is true: Bloom will make a round-trip from home and back, while Stephen will set forth from the Martello Tower but will not return there. In order for Bloom's circular trip to resemble Odysseus's one-way trip, his home must be compared both to Calypso's island, in this chapter, and to Ithaca, in the final two chapters (Ithaca and Penelope). Molly Bloom, then, plays two roles, as temptress and wife. These twin roles emphasize both her complexity of character and the fact that, for Bloom, all women are but types of Molly.

CHAPTER 5: LOTUS EATERS

Bloom goes to the Westland Row post office, where he picks up a letter from Martha Clifford, with whom he has been carrying on a clandestine correspondence under the name Henry Flower. He meets M'Coy, who delays Bloom's reading of Martha's letter; enters a church and watches the service; goes to a pharmacy to order a lotion for Molly (and picks up a bar of lemon-scented soap, which he plans to pay for when he returns for the lotion); and is accosted by Bantam Lyons, who asks to see the racing section of Bloom's newspaper.

After leaving Troy for Ithaca, Odysseus and his men face a series of dangers or challenges. One of the first threats comes from the Lotus Eaters, a passive, indolent people whose fruit causes anyone eating it to become apathetic and unwilling to exert himself. The theme is suggested in *Ulysses* in a variety of ways, including Bloom's thoughts about impotence and the use of vegetative imagery.

CHAPTER 6: HADES

This episode is concerned with Bloom's trip to Glasnevin Cemetery for the burial of his friend Paddy Dignam, who died earlier in the week. Also in the funeral carriage are Simon Dedalus (Stephen's father), Martin Cunningham, and Jack Power. The carriage passes Stephen Dedalus, whom Bloom sees (but Simon doesn't); Boylan, whom Bloom avoids looking at; and Reuben J. Dodd, a moneylender. From Bloom's thoughts and from what Cunningham tells Simon, we learn that Bloom's father committed suicide some years back and that Bloom makes a trip to Ennis, in County Clare, each year on the anniversary of his father's death, 27 June. At the funeral Bloom sees, then loses sight of, an unidentified man wearing a mackintosh; when Bloom refers to the man's coat, Joe Hynes thinks he is referring to his name and writes down the man's name as M'Intosh.

The order of episodes in *Ulysses* differs from that of the *Odyssey*, for Odysseus visits Hades after his sojourn on Circe's island, whereas the Circe chapter of *Ulysses* takes place much later than Hades. Like Odysseus, however, Bloom will emerge with a new sense of life after this encounter with the dead.

CHAPTER 7: AEOLUS

Bloom is a free-lance advertising canvasser, and in this episode his job takes him to the newspaper offices where he is negotiating for an advertisement for Alexander Keyes, Wine and Spirits Merchant. Stephen also appears in the chapter, having come to the newspaper to place Mr. Deasy's letter, but Stephen and Bloom do not yet meet. Among the hangers-on in the office, much of the discussion concerns political oratory. At the end of the chapter, Stephen tells his "Parable of the Plums," whose simple style, inconclusiveness, and emphasis on failure constitute an answer to patriotic rhetoric.

In the *Odyssey*, Aeolus is the keeper of the winds. Here, windiness is suggested not only by actual breezes but also by the focus on rhetoric, an emphasis underscored by the bold-faced headings, or "head-lines," which satirize the overblown style of modern journalism.

CHAPTER 8: LESTRYGONIANS

Bloom meets Josie Breen, who tells him that Mina Purefoy has been in labor for three days. Bloom considers eating lunch at the Burton, but is repelled by the "dirty eaters" there; he then goes to Davy Byrnes's pub, where he has a glass of burgundy and a cheese sandwich and engages in conversation with Nosey Flynn. His plan is to go to the library to copy the Keyes ad from a Kilkenny newspaper, but at chapter's end he veers off toward the museum in order to avoid meeting Boylan.

Homer's Lestrygonians are cannibalistic giants, and their crude-ness is suggested by the eaters in the Burton. Eating is a major theme of the chapter.

CHAPTER 9: SCYLLA AND CHARYBDIS

At the National Library, Stephen unveils his Hamlet theory to a group that includes George Russell (AE), John Eglinton, the librarian, Mr. Lyster, and his assistant, Mr. Best. Stephen's theory, unlike others that he raises and dismisses, identifies Shakespeare primarily with the Ghost of Hamlet's father, rather than with the Prince, an interpreta-tion that allows Stephen to develop a complex association between paternity and artistic creation. Toward the end of the chapter, Mulli-gan joins the group and mocks Stephen's theory. As they leave the library, Mulligan and Stephen pass Leopold Bloom.

Scylla and Charybdis—the monster and the whirlpool between which Odysseus steers his ship—may be roughly equated with compet-ing interpretations of *Hamlet*. Navigating between the extremes of Aristotelian realism and Platonic idealism, Stephen steers closer to realism, founding his theory on an identification of life and art, but immediately distances himself from his own theory when asked if he believes it. By associating the artist figure with a Bloom-like father and cuckold, and figuratively playing the Odyssean role himself, Stephen unconsciously moves toward the maturity represented by Leopold Bloom.

CHAPTER 10: WANDERING ROCKS

This chapter is divided into nineteen sections. The first eighteen focus on individual Dubliners, giving us a series of glimpses into their midday activities; the last section reviews the Dublin street scene, as it follows the procession of the Lord Lieutenant's party from the viceregal lodge in Phoenix Park toward the opening of the Mirus Bazaar in Ballsbridge. Thoughout the chapter, parts of these disparate narratives are interpolated into other narratives, often with ironic effect. Bloom and Stephen are present in this chapter (both, significantly, at bookstalls), but neither is the center of the chapter's attention, as Joyce places his characters within the context of Dublin's urban landscape.

In the *Odyssey*, Odysseus is given the choice of two routes: one will take him past Scylla and Charybdis, the other through the Wandering Rocks. Odysseus avoids the Wandering Rocks, but Joyce sends his hero through them anyway. The characters of the episode are, symbolically, the rocks who wander about Dublin, and much is made of the idea of the characters' bumping into one another—figuratively, as when Lenehan refers to having "knocked against [met up with] Bantam Lyons"; literally, when Cashel Boyle O'Connor Fitzmaurice Tisdall Farrell's dustcoat "brushed rudely from its angle" the blind stripling's cane; and through narrative interventions that move us temporarily from one narrative to another.

CHAPTER 11: SIRENS

Wandering Rocks concludes with the processional scene, which serves as a coda that recapitulates many of the chapter's major themes in addition to reviewing most of its significant characters. The review is essentially spatial, visual, geographical. Sirens reverses these tendencies, beginning with an overture of its chapter's most memorable verbal motifs which exist, in the chapter's opening pages, merely as a series of sounds and words, taken out of context and therefore deprived of meaning. As the chapter proceeds, however, the motifs reappear and gain significance. The action of the chapter centers on the Ormond bar, where Boylan stops before his assignation with Molly. Bloom follows him in, sitting in the next room and eating an early supper with Richie Goulding, Stephen's maternal uncle. After Boylan leaves, Bloom remains, listening to singing from the next room, before resuming his odyssey through Dublin.

The Sirens of the *Odyssey* are temptresses whose enchanting song lures sailors to their death. Odysseus plugged his sailors' ears with wax to make them impervious to the Sirens' song, but had himself tied to the mast so he could hear the song without endangering the ship. Dublin's temptresses are flirtatious barmaids, but the real danger probably lies in the sentimental and patriotic songs sung by Simon Dedalus and the other drinkers. Like Aeolus and Cyclops, this chapter satirizes the rhetoric of nationalism, and it concludes with Bloom's burgundy-induced fart as he reads the last words of the condemned patriot Robert Emmet.

CHAPTER 12: CYCLOPS

This is the only chapter of *Ulysses* narrated in the first person, and even that narration is interrupted from time to time as Joyce halts the narrative proper in order to introduce extravagant parodies of various prose styles. The chapter takes place in Barney Kiernan's pub, where Bloom intends to meet with Martin Cunningham and other friends of Paddy Dignam to arrange for the payment of Dignam's insurance to his widow. By the time Cunningham arrives, Bloom has become embroiled in a political argument with the Citizen—an ardent Irish nationalist—and has left for the courthouse; while he is gone, the rumor spreads that he has won money by betting on Throwaway, the twenty-to-one outsider that won the Ascot Gold Cup race earlier that day. When he returns, Bloom responds aggressively to anti-Semitic slurs, and his exit from the bar—in fact, a somewhat comic affair—is inflated into an event of epic proportions.

The Cyclops is a one-eyed giant who traps Odysseus' men in his cave and eats a number of them before Odysseus puts out the giant's eye with a red-hot, sharpened stake. Earlier, Odysseus told the Cyclops that his name was "Nobody," but as he escapes, he cannot resist telling his real name; the Cyclops then throws a boulder at Odysseus' ship, nearly sinking it. Joyce's Citizen, who lives in the narrow cave of his nationalism, is modeled after the one-eyed Cyclops, although on a greatly reduced scale (he throws a biscuit tin, rather than a boulder, after Bloom), and the chapter is filled with images of vision and blinding, from the opening paragraph where the narrator complains of a chimney sweeper who "near drove his gear into my eye" as he rounded a corner. Although Bloom plays the part of Odysseus, even dramatically waving a cigar (although without aggressive intentions), it is the narrator who is "Nobody" in this chapter, for his identity is never revealed.

CHAPTER 13: NAUSICAA

The first half of this chapter, which takes place on Sandymount Strand, is narrated from the viewpoint of Gerty MacDowell, a somewhat romantic (and, we discover, lame) young woman; the second half gives us Leopold Bloom's perspective. The two halves converge in the middle as Gerty leans back to watch fireworks from the Mirus Bazaar, deliberately lifting her leg to expose her panties to Bloom's view, and Bloom responds by surreptitiously masturbating. The juxtaposition of viewpoints and styles is one of the book's many examples of parallactic technique.

Nausicaa, in Homer's poem, is a Phaeacian princess who discovers Odysseus on the beach and treats him hospitably, partly out of kindness and partly because she is romantically attracted to him. Joyce undercuts the romantic element here through the sentimental prose style that colors Gerty's half of the chapter, and also through Bloom's masturbation, which contrasts strangely with Odysseus's gallantry. The scene also serves as an ironic recapitulation of the bird-girl sequence in chapter 4 of *A Portrait of the Artist as a Young Man*.

CHAPTER 14: OXEN OF THE SUN

In Lestrygonians, Mrs. Breen told Bloom that their friend Mrs. Purefoy has been in labor at the maternity hospital for three days, so in this chapter Bloom goes to the hospital to inquire into her condition. While waiting for her to give birth (she has a boy), Bloom joins a group of revelers, including Stephen Dedalus, who are having a party in the reception room. As pub closing time (11:00 P.M.) nears, they rush out to Burke's pub for drinks. As the chapter ends, Stephen and Lynch make their way to Nighttown or Monto, the Dublin red-light district; Bloom, who is worried about Stephen, follows.

Homer tells us that Odysseus' men killed and ate one of the cattle sacred to Hyperion, the sun god, and for this reason they were all destroyed; because Odysseus had specifically warned them against this sacrilege, however, he was saved. Joyce interprets the killing of the cattle as a crime against fertility, and associates it with the crude talk, by medical students and others, about procreation and contraception. Stylistically, the chapter begins with an imitation of Latinate style, then moves to parodies of English prose styles from Old English through late Victorian and into the melange of competing voices in the modern world. This stylistic pattern is an example of embryonic development.

CHAPTER 15: CIRCE

Stephen and Lynch go to Nighttown, and Bloom locates them in a brothel run by Bella Cohen. Stephen drunkenly imagines that he sees his mother's ghost, and swings his ashplant at a chandelier to exorcise the spirit; as he runs out of the house, Bloom pays for the damages and follows Stephen, only to find him engaged in an argument with a British soldier who eventually knocks him down. The chapter concludes with Bloom watching over the fallen Stephen, whom he associates with his dead son Rudy.

This is by far the longest chapter of *Ulysses,* yet the narration of actual events is brief. Much of the chapter is devoted to a series of fantastic sequences involving parodic transformations, but the precise relationship of these scenes to the book's realistic action is hard to determine: Stephen's vision of his mother appears to be a real hallucination, and Bloom's vision of Rudy might be another, but the remaining visionary events seem to happen on another narrative level altogether. The reader's difficulties in differentiating between the "real" and the "unreal" in this chapter are appropriate in an episode devoted to magic and named after the sorceress and goddess who turns Odysseus' men into swine. The theme of bestiality emerges in various ways, most obviously in the chapter's setting in the brothel district.

CHAPTER 16: EUMAEUS

Bloom takes Stephen to a cabman's shelter where he hopes to get him to eat. There, they meet a man who gives his name as D. B. Murphy, a sailor returning home after a long absence. Bloom and Stephen discuss politics and other subjects, but with little agreement or mutual understanding. Bloom invites Stephen to his house.

When Odysseus returns to Ithaca, in disguise, he first stays at the hut of Eumaeus, a swineherd and a loyal subject. There, he meets Telemachus and plans his revenge on his wife's suitors. In *Ulysses,* we have two versions of Odysseus in the Eumaeus episode: Bloom, the "true" hero, and Murphy, the homeward-bound sailor who may be in disguise (there is some evidence that Murphy is not his real name) and who, like Homer's hero, tells a string of lies to protect his identity. The role of Eumaeus is played by the manager of the shelter, who is reputed to have been implicated in the Phoenix Park murders (1882).

CHAPTER 17: ITHACA

Stephen and Bloom go to Bloom's house at 7 Eccles Street, where Bloom discovers that he has forgotten his key and must enter by climbing over the area railings and dropping down. Letting Stephen in, he engages him in conversation and gives him cocoa. Although Bloom invites Stephen to spend the night, Stephen demurs, and Bloom escorts him out. Returning into the house, Bloom finds some things changed from that morning: the furniture has been moved (he hits his head against a walnut sideboard) and there are crumbs in bed, a sign of Boylan's presence there. Molly asks Bloom about his day, and he gives her a doctored account of his activities. The chapter ends with Bloom (presumably) falling asleep.

The parallel sequence of events in the *Odyssey* involves Odysseus' return home to Ithaca, his slaying of the suitors, and his reconciliation with Penelope. Here, the return is less obviously heroic: Bloom slays no one (although the reader and Molly alike see him as a better man than Boylan), and whereas Odysseus returned to a faithful wife, symbolized by an unmovable bed, Bloom returns to an unfaithful wife, relocated furniture, and an uncertain marital future. Note that the chapter's catechistic format, usually associated with utter certainty, is undercut by various errors as well as by Bloom's human fallibility.

CHAPTER 18: PENELOPE

Throughout *Ulysses*, we have seen Molly Bloom only through Bloom's thoughts and through the conversations of various men. Now, we see the world—and Bloom—from her perspective, as *Ulysses* concludes with a chapter-long interior monologue that gives us direct access to Molly's rambling but energetic mind. Organized into eight paragraphs

Appendix: An Outline of Ulysses

(with periods at the ends of the fourth and eighth paragraphs, but otherwise unpunctuated), Molly's thoughts cover her girlhood in Gibraltar, her sexual encounter that afternoon with Boylan, her upcoming concert trip to Belfast, and the possibility of an affair with Stephen, among other subjects. Her most common subject is Bloom, whom she regards with a mixture of contempt, exasperation, wonderment, and genuine admiration. The book concludes with Molly's recollection of Bloom's proposal and her acceptance.

Homer's Penelope was famous for her fidelity, although other versions of the legend tell of an unfaithful Penelope. Joyce's modern Penelope combines aspects of these two models: she has begun an affair with Boylan but has no intention of leaving Bloom. The chapter is carefully balanced in every way, and an intricate design lies under the appearance of randomness and disorder, just as it does throughout *Ulysses*. As is typical of Joyce's fiction, the ending of *Ulysses* is ambiguous, and despite the fact that the book concludes with an emphatic "Yes," there is no evidence that Molly will make Bloom's breakfast for him.

Notes

Preface

1. Gerald L. Bruns, *Inventions: Writing, Textuality, and Understanding in Literary History* (New Haven, Conn.: Yale University Press, 1982), 161.
2. Ibid., 165.

Chapter 1

1. Dominic Manganiello, *Joyce's Politics* (London: Routledge & Kegan Paul, 1980), 98.
2. Douglas Hyde, "The Necessity for De-Anglicising Ireland," in *1000 Years of Irish Prose*, ed. Vivian Mercier and David H. Greene (New York: Grosset & Dunlap, 1961), 84, 89.
3. Seamus Deane, *Celtic Revivals: Essays in Modern Irish Literature, 1880–1980* (Winston-Salem, N. C.: Wake Forest University Press, 1987), 92.

Chapter 2

1. Samuel Beckett, *Proust* (1931; reprint, New York: Grove Press, 1957), 67. Cf. Beckett's comment that in *Work in Progress* (later *Finnegans Wake*), "Here form *is* content, content *is* form. . . . [Joyce's] writing is not *about* something: *it is that something itself.*" "Dante... Bruno. Vico.. Joyce," in *Our Exagmination Round his Factification for Incamination of Work in Progress* (1929; reprint, New York: New Directions, 1972), 14.
2. José Ortega y Gasset, "The Dehumanization of Art," in *The Dehumanization of Art and Other Essays on Art, Culture, and Literature* (Princeton, N. J.: Princeton University Press, 1968).
3. Breon Mitchell, *James Joyce and the German Novel 1922–1933* (Athens: Ohio University Press, 1976); Vivian Mercier, *The New Novel from Queneau to Pinget* (New York: Farrar, Straus and Giroux, 1971), 23.

Notes

4. Robert Martin Adams, *After Joyce: Studies in Fiction After "Ulysses"* (New York: Oxford University Press, 1977).

Chapter 3

1. Richard M. Kain, *Fabulous Voyager: A Study of James Joyce's "Ulysses,"* rev. ed. (New York: Viking Press, 1959), 35.

2. Hugh Kenner, *Dublin's Joyce* (Bloomington: Indiana University Press, 1956), 11.

3. Ibid., 12.

4. Stanley Sultan, "The Adventures of *Ulysses* in Our World," in *Joyce's "Ulysses": The Larger Perspective*, ed. Robert D. Newman and Weldon Thornton (Newark: University of Delaware Press, 1987), 271–310; also revised as chapter 10 of Sultan, *Eliot, Joyce and Company* (New York: Oxford University Press, 1987), 262–301.

Chapter 4

1. David Hayman, *"Ulysses": The Mechanics of Meaning*, rev. ed. (Madison: University of Wisconsin Press, 1982), 88–104, 117, 122–25; also, Hayman, "Cyclops," in *James Joyce's "Ulysses": Critical Essays*, ed. Clive Hart and David Hayman (Berkeley and Los Angeles: University of California Press, 1974), 265–66.

2. Cf. Sheldon Brivic's argument that "the realistic narrator and the inventive arranger Hayman distinguishes are not two people, but poles of one mind" (*Joyce the Creator* [Madison: University of Wisconsin Press, 1985], 85).

3. My position here is substantially in agreement with the one set forth by Weldon Thornton in "Voices and Values in *Ulysses*," in *Joyce's "Ulysses": The Larger Perspective*, ed. Robert D. Newman and Weldon Thornton, 244–70.

4. Marilyn French, *The Book as World: James Joyce's "Ulysses"* (Cambridge, Mass.: Harvard University Press, 1976), 87.

5. Laurence Sterne, *The Life and Opinions of Tristram Shandy, Gentleman*, ed. James Aiken Work (New York: Odyssey Press, 1940), 218.

6. For other connections between Bloom's interior monologue and events that Bloom cannot have seen or heard, see Paul van Caspel, *Bloomers on the Liffey: Eisegetical Readings of Joyce's "Ulysses"* (Baltimore: Johns Hopkins University Press, 1986), 161–62.

7. Hugh Kenner, *The Pound Era* (Berkeley and Los Angeles: University of California Press, 1971), 37.

8. Kenner, *"Ulysses"* (London: George Allen & Unwin, 1980), 55–56; Fritz Senn, "Righting *Ulysses,*" in *James Joyce: New Perspectives,* ed. Colin MacCabe (Bloomington: Indiana University Press, 1982), 17; van Caspel, *Bloomers on the Liffey,* 28–30; Heather Cook Callow, "Exiles, Keys, and Salt Bread: Yet Another Note on Who Rented the Tower," *James Joyce Quarterly* 22 (Summer 1985): 425–27. Kenner traces his reading of the passage to a suggestion made by Arnold Goldman.

9. Karen Lawrence, *The Odyssey of Style in "Ulysses"* (Princeton, N.J.: Princeton University Press, 1981), 62, 64.

10. Marilyn French, "Joyce and Language," *James Joyce Quarterly* 19 (Spring 1982): 240, 253.

Chapter 5

1. Phillip F. Herring, *Joyce's Uncertainty Principle* (Princeton, N.J.: Princeton University Press, 1987), 93.

2. Robert Martin Adams, *Surface and Symbol: The Consistency of James Joyce's "Ulysses"* (New York: Oxford University Press, 1962), 21. See Adams, 18–26, for a thorough analysis of Deasy's historical errors.

3. On the Limerick incident, which figures in the background of *Ulysses,* see Marvin Magalaner, "The Anti-Semitic Limerick Incidents and Joyce's 'Bloomsday,' " *PMLA* 48 (December 1953):1219–23, and Louis Hyman, *The Jews of Ireland from Earliest Times to the Year 1910* (Shannon: Irish University Press, 1972), 212–17.

4. Zack Bowen, *Musical Allusions in the Works of James Joyce: Early Poetry through "Ulysses"* (Albany: State University of New York Press, 1974), 99, 210, 317. Bloom's confusion of Mercadante and Meyerbeer explains his surprising identification of Mercadante as a Jew (12.1804/342).

5. Shari Benstock and Bernard Benstock, *Who's He When He's at Home: A James Joyce Directory* (Urbana: University of Illinois Press, 1980), 229–33.

6. Weldon Thornton, *Allusions in "Ulysses": An Annotated List* (Chapel Hill: University of North Carolina Press, 1968), 14.

7. Toward the end of Oxen of the Sun, in the mingling of voices at Burke's pub, someone says, "Mummer's wire. Cribbed out of Meredith. Jesified, orchidised, polycimical jesuit! Aunty mine's writing Pa Kinch. Baddybad Stephen lead astray goodygood Malachi" (14.1486–88/425). If this is Mulligan speaking, rather than Stephen mimicking him, then Mulligan now knows that Stephen "cribbed" his telegram from Meredith, but the text does

not tell us whether Mulligan instantly recognized the reference or had it pointed out to him later in the day, perhaps by Stephen.

8. Brook Thomas, *James Joyce's "Ulysses": A Book of Many Happy Returns* (Baton Rouge: Louisiana State University Press, 1982), 165–66.

9. Denis Donoghue, *The Arts without Mystery* (Boston: Little, Brown, 1983), 12.

10. Herring, *Joyce's Uncertainty Principle*, 108–17.

11. Clive Hart and Leo Knuth, *A Topographical Guide to James Joyce's "Ulysses"* (Colchester, England: A Wake Newslitter Press, 1975), 14.

Chapter 6

1. Kenner, *"Ulysses,"* 103.

2. Bloom's reference to "twenty odd years" in this passage is sometimes misread as a reference to how long he thinks Parnell has been dead: see, for example, John Henry Raleigh, "On the Way Home to Ithaca: The Functions of the 'Eumaeus' Section in *Ulysses*," *Irish Renaissance Annual* 2 (1981):40, and Don Gifford and Robert J. Seidman, *Notes for Joyce: An Annotation of James Joyce's "Ulysses"* (New York: E. P. Dutton, 1974), 452. Brook Thomas, in *James Joyce's "Ulysses,"* 79, notes the Parnell-Odysseus connection but curiously misreads the reference to "twenty odd years" as the cabman's statement of how long Parnell's absence will last.

3. Adams, *Surface and Symbol*, 61–64.

4. The confusion of literal and figurative meaning is especially appropriate in Eumaeus, a chapter in which "literally" invariably means "figuratively," as it does in the first line of "The Dead," where Lily is "literally run off her feet." In Eumaeus we have "a thrill went through the packed court literally electrifying everybody" (16.1373–74/651), "Literally astounded at this piece of intelligence Bloom reflected" (16.1578/656), "four coppers, literally the last of the Mohicans" (16.1697–98/660), and "the acme of first class music as such, literally knocking everything else into a cocked hat" (16.1739–40/661). Rumors, Joyce realized, often emerge from mistaking the figurative for the literal.

5. Patricia Meyer Spacks, *Gossip* (New York: Alfred A. Knopf, 1985), 22.

6. Ibid., 168–69.

7. Michael Seidel, *Epic Geography: James Joyce's "Ulysses"* (Princeton, N.J.: Princeton University Press, 1976), 91.

Chapter 7

1. Erwin R. Steinberg, "James Joyce and the Critics Notwithstanding, Leopold Bloom Is Not Jewish," *Journal of Modern Literature* 9 (1981/ 1982):29. Further page references are cited parenthetically.

2. Shari Benstock, "Is He a Jew or a Gentile or a Holy Roman?," *James Joyce Quarterly* 16 (Summer 1979):493.

3. Ellmann (513) says "Joyce had related Bloom" to this Higgins family, but it is unclear whether this statement is derived from Joyce or is merely Ellmann's (or Leventhal's) interpretation. See also Hyman, *The Jews of Ireland,* 143, where Hyman mentions a John (Jacob) Michael Higgins (1874–1916) who converted to Judaism, apparently to marry a Jewish girl, Lillie Marks.

4. Benstock, "Is He a Jew or a Gentile," 495.

5. See Adams, *Surface and Symbol,* 197–98; Thornton, *Allusions in "Ulysses,"* 303; and Steinberg, "James Joyce and the Critics Notwithstanding," 34–35.

6. Jean-Paul Sartre, *Anti-Semite and Jew,* trans. George J. Becker (New York: Schocken Books, 1948), 13, 68, 72. Further page references are cited parenthetically.

7. David Daiches, "James Joyce's Jew," *Jewish Chronicle Quarterly Supplement* (25 December 1959), 2.

8. Hyman, *The Jews of Ireland,* 169.

9. In the 1959 edition of *James Joyce,* Ellmann called Hunter "a dark-complexioned Dublin Jew" and cited an interview with Stanislaus Joyce as his source of information (238, 778 n. 38); in the revised edition Ellmann partially corrected his error, referring to Hunter as "the putatively Jewish Dubliner" (230).

10. Adams, *Surface and Symbol,* 105–6. See also S. L. Goldberg, *The Classical Temper: A Study of James Joyce's "Ulysses"* (London: Chatto and Windus, 1961), 272; Stanley Sultan, *The Argument of "Ulysses"* (Columbus: Ohio State University Press, 1964), 99, 239, 244; Bernard Benstock, *"Ulysses* without Dublin," *James Joyce Quarterly* 10 (Fall 1972):116; French, *The Book as World,* 86; Seidel, *Epic Geography,* 161; Suzette Henke, *Joyce's Moraculous Sindbook: A Study of "Ulysses"* (Columbus: Ohio State University Press, 1978), 102–3; James F. Carens, *Surpassing Wit: Oliver St. John Gogarty, His Poetry and His Prose* (New York: Columbia University Press, 1979), 129; Barbara Reich Gluck, *Beckett and Joyce: Friendship and Fiction* (Lewisburg, Pa.: Bucknell University Press, 1979), 169–70; John Gordon, *James Joyce's Metamorphoses* (Dublin: Gill and Macmillan, 1981), 97; Jackson I. Cope, *Joyce's Cities: Archaeologies of the Soul* (Baltimore: Johns Hopkins University Press, 1981), 25–26, and David Hayman, *"Ulysses": The*

Notes

Mechanics of Meaning, rev. ed. (Madison: University of Wisconsin Press, 1982), 54, 156 n. 4. Benstock and Gordon both hedge their bets, however, Gordon by referring to Dodd as "another (supposed) Jew" and Benstock by arguing that "Those in the funeral carriage who see Reuben J. Dodd assume that he is Jewish; Joyce of course knew that he was not, but allowed his characters the misinformation of a Dublin rumor, a greater reality." Hayman, likewise, maintains that "the historical Dodd was not Jewish, but the text lets us believe along with Dublin that he was." Sultan has corrected his reading; see his *Eliot, Joyce and Company,* 80–81.

11. R. M. Adams, "Hades," in *James Joyce's "Ulysses": Critical Essays,* ed. Clive Hart and David Hayman, 97.

12. Robert Boyle, S.J., "A Note on Reuben J. Dodd as 'a dirty Jew,' " *James Joyce Quarterly* 3 (Fall 1965): 64–66; Boyle, untitled review of *The Book as World* by Marilyn French, *James Joyce Quarterly* 13 (Summer 1976): 484–85; Boyle, "Jackson Cope's Icarian Flight," *Irish Literary Supplement* 1 (Spring 1982):6; Hyman, *The Jews of Ireland,* 164.

13. Adams, "Hades," 97.

14. On "James Wought alias Saphiro alias Spark and Spiro" (12.1086–87/322), see Hyman, *The Jews of Ireland,* 175, 333 n. 88.

15. Boyle, "A Note on Reuben J. Dodd," 66.

16. Adams, "Hades," 97.

17. Ibid., 97.

18. On *Ulysses* as a critique of Irish Literary Renaissance values, see G. J. Watson, "The Politics of *Ulysses,*" in *Joyce's "Ulysses": The Larger Perspective,* ed. Robert D. Newman and Weldon Thornton, 39–58.

19. Stuart Gilbert, *James Joyce's "Ulysses": A Study,* rev ed. (New York: Vintage Books, 1955), 156.

20. Herbert Howarth, *The Irish Writers 1880–1940: Literature under Parnell's Star* (London: Rockcliff, 1958), 24–25.

Chapter 8

1. Joseph Frank, "Spatial Form in Modern Literature," *Sewanee Review* 53 (1945):234.

2. French, *The Book as World,* 3–4.

3. Thomas, *James Joyce's "Ulysses,"* 162–63.

4. Molly's reflection that reading a letter "fills up your whole day" may suggest a link between reading and sexual activity if we associate it with her use of "full up" in "I never in all my life felt anyone had one the size of that to make you feel full up" (18.149–50/742). Similarly, Bloom's question about

Molly's reading—"Did you finish it?" (4.354/64)—seems to foreshadow Molly's repeated use of "finish" to refer to sexual climax (18.99/740, 18.156/742, 18.809/760).

5. Hugh Kenner, *A Colder Eye: The Modern Irish Writers* (New York: Alfred A. Knopf, 1983), 155; Wolfgang Iser, *The Act of Reading; A Theory of Aesthetic Response* (Baltimore: Johns Hopkins University Press, 1978), 84.

6. Kenner, *"Ulysses,"* 53.

7. Sir Philip Sidney, *The Defense of Poesy*, ed. Lewis Soens (Lincoln: University of Nebraska Press, 1970), 7.

8. Kenner, *The Pound Era*, 380.

9. Mary Power, "The Discovery of *Ruby,"* *James Joyce Quarterly* 18 (Winter 1981):115–21.

10. Cf. Bernard Benstock, "Reflections on *Ruby,"* *James Joyce Quarterly* 19 (Spring 1982):340. The name Enrico does not appear in *Ulysses,* but its equivalent may be found when one of the parodies in Cyclops converts Henry Flower into "Senhor Enrique Flor" (12.1288/327).

11. Zack Bowen, "Lizzie Twigg: Gone But Not Forgotten," *James Joyce Quarterly* 6 (Summer 1969):368–70.

12. Bloom typically skims before reading carefully. Thus as he stands in front of the window of the Belfast and Oriental Tea Company, he reads phrases from the tea packets—"choice blend, finest quality, family tea"—while he is occupied in searching for his Henry Flower card hidden inside his hat; then he "read[s] again: choice blend, made of the finest Ceylon brands" (5.17–29/71). In this instance, however, neither reading is complete, for each one contains words that are missing from the other.

13. Bloom also says, of Beaufoy, "And he, a bachelor, how ..." (15.857/460), implying that as a bachelor, Beaufoy cannot write knowledgeably about women. (Bloom's assumption that Beaufoy is a bachelor is apparently based upon Beaufoy's address, given in *Titbits* as "Playgoers' Club, London" [4.503/68].) Like his creator, Bloom believes firmly in the value of personal experience as a basis for fiction, as he shows when, immediately after reading Beaufoy's story, he thinks of a scheme to write a story based on what Molly says in the mornings (4.518.ff./69); similarly, just after thinking of Beaufoy's literary success, Bloom wonders what luck he might have "suppose he were to pen something out of the common groove. ... My Experiences, let us say, *in a Cabman's Shelter*" (16.1229–31/647).

14. Colin MacCabe, *James Joyce and the Revolution of the Word* (New York: Barnes & Noble, 1979), 84.

15. George Steiner, "Literature and Post-History," in *Language and Silence: Essays on Language, Literature, and the Inhuman* (New York: Atheneum, 1967), 383.

Notes

16. Walter J. Ong, *Orality and Literacy: the Technologizing of the Word* (London: Methuen, 1982), 69.

17. Patrick A. McCarthy, "Joyce's Silent Readers," in *New Alliances in Joyce Studies: "When it's Aped to Foul a Delfian,"* ed. Bonnie Kime Scott (Newark, Del.: University of Delaware Press, 1988), 73–78. Other aspects of the present chapter are related to those I have dealt with in *"Ulysses* and the Printed Page," in *Joyce's "Ulysses": The Larger Perspective,* ed. Robert D. Newman and Weldon Thornton, 59–73.

18. Ong, *Orality and Literacy,* 131.

19. Fritz Senn, "Righting *Ulysses,*" in *James Joyce: New Perspectives,* ed. Colin MacCabe, 13.

Bibliography

Primary Works

Joyce's books are arranged according to dates of first publication. Current editions are listed in brackets.

Chamber Music. London: Elkin Mathews, 1907. [In *Collected Poems.* New York: Viking Press, 1957.]

Dubliners. London: Grant Richards, 1914. [*Dubliners: Text, Criticism, and Notes.* Edited by Robert Scholes and A. Walton Litz. Viking Critical Edition. New York: Viking Press, 1969.]

A Portrait of the Artist as a Young Man. New York: B. W. Huebsch. 1916. [*A Portrait of the Artist as a Young Man: Text, Criticism, and Notes.* Edited by Chester G. Anderson. Viking Critical Edition. New York: Viking Press, 1968.]

Exiles: A Play in Three Acts. London: Grant Richards, 1918. [Reprint, with Introduction by Padraic Colum and "Notes by the Author." New York: Viking Press, 1961.]

Ulysses. Paris: Shakespeare and Company, 1922. [*Ulysses,* "corrected and reset" edition. New York: Random House, 1961. *Ulysses: The Corrected Text.* Edited by Hans Walter Gabler. New York: Random House, 1986. The 1986 edition is based on the reading text in *Ulysses: A Critical and Synoptic Edition.* 3 vols. Edited by Hans Walter Gabler. New York and London: Garland Publishing, 1984.]

Pomes Penyeach. Paris: Shakespeare and Company, 1927. [In *Collected Poems.* New York: Viking Press, 1957.]

Finnegans Wake. New York: Viking Press, 1939. [Eighth printing, "with the author's corrections incorporated in the text." New York: Viking Press, 1958.]

Stephen Hero. Edited by Theodore Spencer. Norfolk, Conn.: New Directions,

Bibliography

1944. [New edition, including additional manuscript pages. Edited by John J. Slocum and Herbert Cahoon. New York: New Directions, 1963.]

Letters of James Joyce. 3 vols. Vol. 1 (1957) edited by Stuart Gilbert. Vols. 2 and 3 (1966) edited by Richard Ellmann. New York: Viking Press, 1966.

The Critical Writings of James Joyce. Edited by Richard Ellmann and Ellsworth Mason. New York: Viking Press, 1959.

Giacomo Joyce. Edited by Richard Ellmann. New York: Viking Press, 1968.

Joyce's "Ulysses" Notesheets in the British Museum. Edited by Phillip F. Herring. Charlottesville: University Press of Virginia, 1972.

Selected Letters of James Joyce. Edited by Richard Ellmann. New York: Viking Press, 1975.

Joyce's Notes and Early Drafts for "Ulysses": Selections from the Buffalo Collection. Edited by Phillip F. Herring. Charlottesville: University Press of Virginia, 1977.

The James Joyce Archive. 63 vols. Edited by Michael Groden et al. New York and London: Garland Publishing, 1978.

Secondary Works

This list is limited to selected books dealing with *Ulysses* or with Joyce's work generally.

Adams, Robert Martin. *Surface and Symbol: The Consistency of James Joyce's "Ulysses."* New York: Oxford University Press, 1962. Explores Joyce's use of his source materials.

Bowen, Zack. *Musical Allusions in the Works of James Joyce: Early Poetry through "Ulysses."* Albany: State University of New York Press, 1974. Both a critical study and a reference book.

———*"Ulysses" as a Comic Novel.* Syracuse, N. Y.: Syracuse University Press, 1989. A reading of *Ulysses* in relation to theories of comedy and to the comic tradition of Rabelais, Cervantes, and Sterne.

Bowen, Zack, and James F. Carens, eds. *A Companion to Joyce Studies.* Westport, Conn: Greenwood Press, 1984. Essays on all of Joyce's books and on significant aspects of his life and works.

Brivic, Sheldon. *Joyce the Creator.* Madison: University of Wisconsin Press, 1985. Analyzes Joyce's works as dramatizations of forces and conflicts in their creator's mind.

Budgen, Frank. *James Joyce and the Making of "Ulysses."* 1934; reprinted,

Bloomington: Indiana University Press, 1960. An important study based on Budgen's conversations with Joyce.

Deming, Robert H., ed. *James Joyce: The Critical Heritage,* 2 vols. New York: Barnes & Noble, 1970. Reprinted reviews and early criticism of Joyce's works.

Dunleavy, Janet Egleson, ed. *Classics of Joyce Criticism.* Urbana: University of Illinois Press, 1990. Essays on the original contribution to Joyce scholarship, and continuing influence, of major critical studies published between 1929 and 1960.

Ellmann, Richard. *James Joyce.* 1959; revised, New York: Oxford University Press, 1982. The standard biography.

French, Marilyn. *The Book as World: James Joyce's "Ulysses."* Cambridge, Mass.: Harvard University Press, 1976. Thematic and stylistic analyses of individual chapters.

Gifford, Don, with Robert J. Seidman. *Notes for Joyce: An Annotation of James Joyce's "Ulysses."* New York: Dutton, 1974. An extensive, but sometimes unreliable or misleading, set of glosses. (A revised edition has been announced by the University of California Press.)

Gilbert, Stuart. *James Joyce's "Ulysses": A Study.* 1930; revised, New York: Vintage Books, 1952. The first important full-length study; emphasizes the Homeric parallels.

Goldberg, S. L. *The Classical Temper: A Study of James Joyce's "Ulysses."* London: Chatto and Windus, 1961. A reading of *Ulysses* as a "representational novel."

Goldman, Arnold. *The Joyce Paradox: Form and Freedom in His Fiction.* Evanston, Ill: Northwestern University Press, 1966. Explores the interplay of realistic and symbolic elements in *Dubliners, Portrait,* and *Ulysses.*

Gose, Elliott B., Jr. *The Transformation Process in Joyce's "Ulysses."* Toronto: University of Toronto Press, 1980. A study of Joyce's artistic vision in relation to various kinds of transformation.

Groden, Michael. *"Ulysses" in Progress.* Princeton, N. J.: Princeton University Press, 1977. Shows how the process of composing *Ulysses* reflected Joyce's developing intentions.

Hart, Clive. *James Joyce's "Ulysses."* Sydney: Sydney University Press, 1968. A good introductory study.

Hart, Clive, and David Hayman, eds. *James Joyce's "Ulysses": Critical Essays.* Berkeley and Los Angeles: University of California Press, 1974. Essays by major critics on individual chapters.

Hart, Clive, and Leo Knuth. *A Topographical Guide to James Joyce's "Ulys-*

ses." Colchester, England: A Wake Newslitter Press, 1975. Maps and text emphasizing the importance of Dublin's streets as background to *Ulysses.*

Hayman, David. *"Ulysses": The Mechanics of Meaning.* 1970; revised, Madison: University of Wisconsin Press, 1982. Brief but important analyses of backgrounds, characterization, structure, style, etc.; introduces the concept of the "arranger."

Herr, Cheryl. *Joyce's Anatomy of Culture.* Urbana: University of Illinois Press, 1986. Shows the impact of selected aspects of Dublin culture—the press, the popular stage, and sermons—on Joyce's work.

Herring, Phillip F. *Joyce's Uncertainty Principle.* Princeton: Princeton University Press, 1987. Examines Joyce's use of uncertainty as a thematic and structural element.

Kain, Richard M. *Fabulous Voyager: James Joyce's "Ulysses."* 1947; corrected, New York: Viking Press, 1959. The first book on *Ulysses* to demonstrate the importance of tracing themes and motifs throughout the whole book.

Kenner, Hugh. *Dublin's Joyce.* Bloomington: Indiana University Press, 1956. Emphasizes Joyce's ironic perspective.

———. *Joyce's Voices.* Berkeley and Los Angeles: University of California Press, 1978. A brief, elegant essay on style; introduces the "Uncle Charles Principle."

———. *"Ulysses."* 1980; revised, Baltimore: Johns Hopkins University Press, 1986. Chapter-by-chapter analysis showing how Joyce's book teaches us to read it.

Lawrence Karen. *The Odyssey of Style in "Ulysses."* Princeton, N. J.: Princeton University Press, 1981. Analyzes the evolving styles of *Ulysses.*

Litz, A. Walton. *The Art of James Joyce: Method and Design in "Ulysses" and "Finnegans Wake."* 1961; corrected, London: Oxford University Press, 1964. The first study to make extensive use of unpublished drafts to study Joyce's composition process.

Maddox, James H., Jr. *Joyce's "Ulysses" and the Assault on Character.* New Brunswick, N. J.: Rutgers University Press, 1978. Focuses on Joyce's deviation from traditional characterization.

Manganiello, Dominic. *Joyce's Politics.* London: Routledge & Kegan Paul, 1980. Joyce's response to Irish and European political events.

Newman, Robert D., and Weldon Thornton, eds. *James Joyce's "Ulysses": The Larger Perspective.* Newark: University of Delaware Press, 1987. Broad-ranging essays emphasizing holistic approaches to *Ulysses.*

Raleigh, John Henry. *The Chronicle of Leopold and Molly Bloom: "Ulysses" as Narrative.* Berkeley and Los Angeles: University of California Press,

1977. The events of the Blooms' family history treated in chronological order.

Schutte, William M. *Joyce and Shakespeare: A Study in the Meaning of "Ulysses."* New Haven, Conn.: Yale University Press, 1957. Attempts to relate Joyce's, and Stephen's, use of Shakespeare to their aesthetics.

Seidel, Michael. *Epic Geography: James Joyce's "Ulysses."* Princeton, N.J.: Princeton University Press, 1976. Shows the relevance of Victor Berard's *Les Phéneciens et l'Odyssée* to *Ulysses,* but probably pushes too far the parallels between geographical directions in *Ulysses* and in the *Odyssey.*

Staley, Thomas F., and Bernard Benstock, eds. *Approaches to "Ulysses": Ten Essays.* Pittsburgh: University of Pittsburgh Press, 1970. Essays on Joyce's techniques, sources, and characters.

Sultan, Stanley, *The Argument of "Ulysses."* Columbus: Ohio State University Press, 1964. Emphasizes the book's human element.

———. *Eliot, Joyce and Company.* New York: Oxford University Press, 1987. Demonstrates the values underlying modernist experiments in presenting the interplay of mind and world.

Theoharis, Theoharis Constantine. *Joyce's "Ulysses": An Anatomy of the Soul.* Chapel Hill: University of North Carolina Press, 1988. Joyce's concept of the soul in *Ulysses,* seen in the light of Aristotle, Bruno, Dante, and Arnold.

Thomas, Brook. *James Joyce's "Ulysses": A Book of Many Happy Returns.* Baton Rouge: Louisiana State University Press, 1982. Studies the idea of return as both theme and technique in *Ulysses.*

Thornton, Weldon. *Allusions in "Ulysses": An Annotated List.* Chapel Hill: University of North Carolina Press, 1968. An indispensable reference guide.

Tucker, Lindsey. *Stephen and Bloom at Life's Feast: Alimentary Symbolism and the Creative Process in James Joyce's "Ulysses."* Columbus: Ohio State University Press, 1984. On Joyce's symbolic use of references to eating, digestion, and elimination.

van Caspel, Paul. *Bloomers on the Liffey: Eisegetical Readings of Joyce's "Ulysses."* Baltimore: Johns Hopkins University Press, 1986. Mainly a study of how various critics have interpreted (and misinterpreted) specific passages.

Index

Adams, Robert Martin, 12, 20, 57, 78, 79, 80, 83, 128
Agendath Netaim flyer, 106–7
Aldington, Richard, 14–15
Ananais, 48
Aristotle's *Masterpiece*, 109
Augustine, St.: *Confessions*, 98
Austen, Jane: *Emma*, 65–66

Ball, Sir Robert, 29
Barabbas, 79, 81, 82
Barth, John, 12
Baudelaire, Charles: *Les Fleurs du mal*, 110
Beckett, Samuel, 1, 10, 12, 126
bed (Bloom's), 36
Benstock, Bernard, 41, 130–31, 132
Benstock, Shari, 41, 71, 72
Bergson, Henri, 15
Bloom, Harold, 100
Boccaccio: *Decameron*, 63
Borach, Georges, 7
Borges, Jorge Luis, 12
Bowen, Zack, 39, 103
Boyle, Robert, S.J., 78, 80, 81
Brecht, Bertolt, 11
Brivic, Sheldon, 127
Broch, Hermann, 12
Budgen, Frank, 16–17, 18, 113
Butor, Michel, 12

Caesar, Julius, 11
Callow, Heather Cook, 33
Carens, James F., 130
Carey, James, 47, 102
Claver, Peter, 47
Conrad, Joseph, 1
Cope, Jackson I., 130

Dante Alighieri: *The Divine Comedy*, 69
Deane, Seamus, 7
Defoe, Daniel: *Moll Flanders*, 95, 97, 102; *Robinson Crusoe*, 98
de Kock, Paul, 32, 100
Doblin, Alfred, 12
Dodd, Reuben J., father: 75, 77–83, 117, 131
Dodd, Reuben J., son: 81, 82, 83
Donoghue, Denis, 46
Dumas, Alexandre: *The Count of Monte Cristo*, 55
Dunsink vs. Greenwich Time, 29, 39, 88

Eglinton, John, 103, 118
Einstein, Albert, 15
Eliot, T. S., 1, 11; "*Ulysses*, Order and Myth," 15, 94; *The Waste Land*, 15, 22, 27
Ellmann, Richard, 19, 57, 78, 130
Emmet, Robert, 106, 120

Faulkner, William, 12, 22; *The Sound and the Fury*, 12
"Finnegan's Wake" (song), 55
Finney, Lazarus, 80
Fish, Stanley, 83, 103
Flaubert, Gustave, 3
Frank, Joseph, 95
French, Marilyn, 21, 30, 35, 95, 130
Freud, Sigmund, 15
Fuentes, Carlos: *A Change of Skin*, 12

Gaelic Athletic Association, 85
Gaelic League/Gaelic Revival, 6, 69, 84–85
Gifford, Don, 20, 129
Gilbert, Stuart, 16–17, 18, 89, 113
Gluck, Barbara Reich, 130
Goldberg, S. L., 20, 130
Goldin, Moses, 83
Goldman, Arnold, 128
Gonne, Maud, 88
Gordon, John, 130–31
Gorman, Herbert, 17, 19
Grant, President Ulysses S., 6
Greek theme, 2, 5–7, 16, 29–30, 67, 68–69, 70, 71, 88, 89, 91, 92–93, 101, 104
Gregory, Lady Augusta: *Spreading the News*, 55
Griffith, Arthur, 59–60, 69; *The Resurrection of Hungary*, 60
Groden, Michael, 21

Hanley, Miles L., 17–18
Hart, Clive, 46
Hayman, David, 21, 27, 127, 130, 131
Heisenberg, Werner, 31
Henke, Suzette, 130
Herodotus, 11
Herr, Cheryl, 21
Herrick, Robert, "To Anthea," 36

Herring, Phillip F., 21–22, 37–38, 46
Higgins family, 71, 130
Higgins, John (Jacob) Michael, 130
Homer: *The Odyssey*, 2, 5, 11, 15, 16, 27–28, 29–30, 36, 37, 55, 56, 70, 77, 88, 92–93, 101, 111, 113–25, 129
Howarth, Herbert, 92
Hunter, Alfred, 78, 82, 130
Hyde, Douglas, 6
Hyman, Louis, 78–79, 128, 130, 131

Ibsen, Henrik, 3
"I Had a Little Nut Tree," 58–59
Ingram, John Kells: "The Memory of the Dead," 89
The Irish Homestead, 4
Irish Literary Revival (Renaissance), 3, 6, 69, 85, 92, 131
Irish Literary Theatre, 3
Irish nationalism, 2–3, 6–8, 38, 48, 59–60, 68–70, 84–93, 120–21
Irving, Washington: "Rip Van Winkle," 55
Iser, Wolfgang, 96

Jackson, Holbrook, 94–95, 105
Jahnn, Henny, 12
Jesus, 72, 73, 75, 81, 82
Jewish theme, 2, 6–7, 38, 46, 54, 60, 64, 67, 69, 70–83, 88–89, 91, 92–93, 114–15, 128, 130–31
Joyce, James, other works by: "The Boarding House," 61; "The Day of the Rabblement," 3, 69; "The Dead," 84, 129; *Dubliners*, 3–5, 38, 96; "An Encounter," "Eveline," 33; *Finnegans Wake*, 7, 16, 17, 41, 53, 99, 111, 126; "Grace," 59, 74, 78, 80; "The Holy Office," 3; "Ire-

Index

land, Island of Saints and Sages," 90–91; "Ivy Day in the Committee Room," 47; "A Little Cloud," 84; "A Mother," 61, 84; *A Portrait of the Artist as a Young Man,* 2, 4, 34, 37, 41, 68, 84, 86, 90, 105, 108, 110, 111, 122; "Two Gallants," 60–61.

Joyce, John Stanislaus (father), 2, 4, 57

Joyce, John Stanislaus (brother), 53, 69, 78, 130

Joyce, Mary Jane Murray (mother), 4

Joyce, Nora Barnacle (wife), 5

Judas Iscariot, 79, 80, 81, 82

Kain, Richard M., 17–18

Kane, Matthew, 57, 58

Kenner, Hugh, 18–19, 21, 33, 53, 96, 98, 101, 128

Knuth, Leo, 46

Lamb, Charles: *The Adventures of Ulysses,* 69

Laubenstein, Arthur, 9

Lawrence, Karen, 21, 34

Leventhal, A. J., 71, 130

Levin, Harry, 18

Lewis, Wyndham, 15–16, 19, 30

Linati, Carlo, 70

Litz, A. Walton, 20

Lowry, Malcolm: *Under the Volcano,* 12, 99

MacCabe, Colin, 107

Magalaner, Marvin, 128

Mailer, Norman, 13

Manganiello, Dominic, 2

Marks, Lillie, 130

Marx, Karl, 73

Maunsel and Co. (publisher), 3

Mauriac, Claude, 12

Mendelssohn, Felix, 73

Mercadante, Saverio, 47, 73, 128; *Seven Last Words of Christ,* 39

Mercier, Vivian, 12

Meredith, George: *The Ordeal of Richard Feverel,* 42, 128–29

metempsychosis, 29–30, 69, 100–101, 102, 103–4, 112

Meyerbeer, Giacomo, 39, 47, 128

Milton, John: *Paradise Lost,* 83

Mitchell, Breon, 12

Moore, Thomas: "Oh! Where's the Slave, So Lowly," 89

Mozart, Wolfgang Amadeus: *Don Giovanni,* 39

Murray, William, 55–57, 58

Nabokov, Vladimir, 1, 12

names, 2, 32–33, 45, 46–48, 57–58, 68–69, 71, 79, 80, 84, 89, 102, 109

Nemo, Captain, 11

O'Casey, Sean, 1

Odysseus: *See* Homer

Ong, Walter, 107–8, 109

Ortega y Gasset, Jose, 12

O'Shea, Kitty, 2, 58–59

Ovid: *Metamorphoses,* 104

parallax, 5, 28–30, 39, 88, 93, 121

Parnell, Charles Stewart, 2–3, 55–56, 57–58, 84, 129

Petrarch, Francesco, 98

Phoenix Park murders, 61–62, 102, 124

Plumtree's Potted Meat, 97, 109

Pound, Ezra, 1, 11, 103

Power, Mary, 101–3

Presley, Elvis, 55

Proust, Marcel, 10

Pynchon, Thomas, 12

Queneau, Raymond, 12

Raleigh, John Henry, 129
Reade, Amye: *Ruby. A Novel,* 101–3
Richards, Grant (publisher), 4, 96
Ruby: the Pride of the Ring, 100–103
Russell, George, 65, 103, 118

Sacher-Masoch, Leopold von: *Venus in Furs,* 103
Sartre, Jean-Paul, 76–77
Seidel, Michael, 21, 66, 130
Senn, Fritz, 21, 33, 110
Shakespeare, John, 63
Shakespeare, William, 63, 91, 96, 99–100, 106; *Hamlet,* 11, 39, 41, 65, 87, 99, 118; *Troilus and Cressida,* 69; *The Winter's Tale,* 55
"The Shan Van Vocht" (song), 85–86, 87–88
Shaw, George Bernard, 1
Sidney, Sir Philip: *The Defense of Poesy,* 98
Sinn Fein, 52, 53, 59–60, 69
Sophocles: *Oedipus Rex,* 55
Sortes Virgilianae, 98–99
Spacks, Patricia Meyer, 65–66
Spinoza, Baruch, 73
Stein, Gertrude, 1
Steinberg, Erwin R., 70–75
Steiner, George, 107
Sterne, Laurence: *Tristram Shandy,* 30
Sultan, Stanley, 20–21, 130, 131
Surprised by Sin: See Fish, Stanley
Sweets of Sin, 98, 106
Swinburne, Algernon Charles, 11
Synge, John M., 89; *In the Shadow of the Glen,* 55; *The Playboy of the Western World,* 55

Taylor, John F., 92
Tennyson, Alfred Lord: "Enoch Arden," 98–99; "Ulysses," 69

Thomas, Brook, 21, 44, 95, 129
Thom's Dublin Post Office Directory, 17–18, 46
Thornton, Weldon, 20, 42, 127
Tindall, William York, 18
Tolstoy, Leo, 3

Ulysses, characters in:
Bannon, Alec, 42–43
Beaufoy, Philip ("Matcham's Masterstroke"), 47, 104–5, 110, 132
Bergan, Alf, 55–57, 66, 76
Best, Richard, 118
blind stripling, 119
Bloom, Milly, 43, 104, 115
Bloom, Molly, 5, 6, 10, 11, 28–29, 31–33, 34, 36, 37, 40, 41, 48, 58, 59, 62–63, 64–65, 71–72, 74, 95–96, 97, 100, 102, 103, 115–16, 120, 124–25, 131–32
Bloom, Rudolph (Virag), 71, 89, 117
Bloom, Rudy, 40, 64, 81, 123
Bloom the dentist, 59
Boylan, Hugh ("Blazes"), 28–29, 31, 32, 33, 47, 64, 104, 115, 117, 118, 120, 125
Breen, Denis, 64, 66
Breen, Josie, 47, 118, 122
Bridgeman, 53, 81
Burke, O'Madden, 61
Burke, Pisser, 64
Carr, Private, 36, 87, 88, 123
cat, Bloom's, 28, 100
Citizen, the, 10–11, 28, 52, 61, 64, 70, 73, 74, 75, 76, 79, 81–82, 89–90, 91, 92, 93, 109, 120–21
Clifford, Martha, 47, 49–50, 51, 109, 110, 116
Cohen, Bella, 122
Corley, John, 60–61

Index

Costello, Punch, 80
Crawford, Myles, 86–87, 106
Crofton, 47–48
Cunningham, Martin, 26, 47–48,
  52, 57, 59, 60, 75, 79, 80, 83,
  117, 120
Cyclops narrator, 40, 47–48, 53–
  54, 61, 64–65, 76, 90, 121
Deasy, Garrett, 38, 70, 106, 114–
  15, 117, 128
Dedalus, May Goulding, 86,
  122–23
Dedalus, Simon, 26, 31–32, 34,
  68, 80, 83, 91, 117, 120
de Kock, Paul, 32, 100
Dignam, Master Patrick, 108–9
Dignam, Paddy, 26, 44, 45, 46,
  53, 55–57, 58, 60, 61, 74, 81,
  82, 109, 117, 120
Dixon, Dr., 64
Dlugacz, Moses, 106
Dodd, Reuben J. (father), 75, 77–
  83, 117, 131
Dodd, Reuben J. (son), 81, 82, 83
Dollard, Ben, 31–32, 82
Doran, Bob, 56–57, 61
Dowie, Dr. John Alexander, 97–
  98, 106
Eglinton, John, 118
Falkiner, Sir Frederick, 79–80, 81
Farrell, Cashel Boyle O'Connor
  Fitzmaurice Tisdall, 34–35, 59,
  119
Figatner, Aaron, 80
Findlater, Adam, 80
Fitzharris, James ("Skin-the-
  Goat"), 61–62, 124
Flower, Henry, 47, 102, 110, 116,
  132
Flynn, Nosey, 118
Goulding, Richie, 57, 66, 110,
  115, 120
Griffith, Arthur, 59–60, 69
Haines, 1, 41, 42, 85–86, 114

Hegarty, Fanny, 71
Higgins, Ellen, 71, 72
Higgins, Julius (Karoly), 71
Holohan, Hoppy, 61
Hynes, Joe, 44–45, 46, 52, 56, 64,
  79, 81, 90, 117
Kane, Matthew, 57, 58
Kelleher, Corny, 89
Kernan, Tom, 74
Keyes, Alexander, 117, 118
Lambert, Ned, 74, 90
Laredo, Lunita, 71–72
Lenehan, 31, 52, 53–55, 57, 82,
  119
Leonard, Paddy, 61
Lynch, Vincent, 122
Lyons, Bantam, 43–44, 48, 55,
  109, 116, 119
Lyster, Thomas William, 118
MacDowell, Gerty, 40, 121–22
MacHugh, Professor, 92
M'Carthy, Jakes, 86–87
M'Coy, C. P., 44–45, 46, 61, 116
milkwoman, 41, 85–86, 87, 114
M'Intosh, 43, 44, 45–46, 48, 117
Mitchell, Susan, 103
Mulligan, Malachi ("Buck"), 5–6,
  7, 11, 25, 41–43, 63–64, 68,
  72, 80, 82, 85–86, 88, 91, 92,
  111, 114, 118, 128–29
Mulvey, Harry, 6
Murphy, D. B., 55, 62, 68, 123
Murray, Willy, 55–57, 58
Nannetti, Joseph Patrick, 91
Nolan, John Wyse, 52, 59, 90
Old Gummy Granny, 87–88
Power, Jack, 26, 48, 56, 79, 117
Purefoy, Mina, 47, 118, 122
Rochford, Tom, 31
Russell, George, 65, 103, 118
Taylor, John F., 92
Throwaway (horse), 43–44, 48,
  54–55, 60, 121
Tweedy, Major (Molly's father), 36

Twigg, Lizzie, 103
Wought, James, 81, 131
Ulysses, episodes in:
Aeolus, 10, 27, 34, 61, 86–87, 91,
  92, 117–18, 120
Calypso, 30, 32, 100–5, 106, 107,
  115–16
Circe, 10, 11, 34, 62, 63–64, 65,
  79, 80, 87–88, 89, 99–100,
  105, 110, 111, 117, 122–23
Cyclops, 10–11, 28, 40, 47–48,
  53–54, 55–57, 59, 60, 61, 64,
  70, 73, 76, 89, 93, 120–21, 132
Eumaeus, 10, 34, 44, 46, 58–59,
  61–62, 68, 74, 75, 81–82,
  123–24, 129
Hades, 26, 44–45, 49, 57, 79,
  117
Ithaca, 10, 34, 39–40, 57, 62–63,
  74, 92, 99, 106, 111, 116, 124
Lestrygonians, 28–29, 32, 34, 49,
  97, 106, 118, 122
Lotus Eaters, 43–44, 49, 74, 116
Nausicaa, 40, 50, 104, 121–22
Nestor, 38, 114–15
Oxen of the Sun, 27, 34, 51, 64,
  122
Penelope, 40, 41, 59, 64–65, 116,
  124–25
Proteus, 48–49, 104, 115
Scylla and Charybdis, 34, 38, 63,
  118–19

Sirens, 10, 30–34, 49, 51, 106,
  110, 119–20
Telemachus, 33, 41–43, 68, 72,
  85–86, 96, 111, 114
Wandering Rocks, 34, 37, 59, 98,
  107–8, 119–20

van Caspel, Paul, 20, 33, 50, 127
Venus in Furs: See Sacher-Masoch,
  Leopold von
Virgil: Aeneid, 69, 98

Wandering Jew, 37, 79, 81, 82, 92
Watson, G. J., 131
Weaver, Harriet Shaw, 52, 103
Wells, H. G., 105
Wilde, Oscar, 1, 41–42; "The Decay
  of Lying," 42; The Picture of
  Dorian Gray, 42
Wilson, Edmund, 18
Woolf, Virginia, 11, 12; Mrs. Dallo-
  way, 12
Wought, James, 81, 131

Yeats, William Butler, 11, 87; Cathleen ni Houlihan, 85, 88; The
  Countess Cathleen, 3; "No Second Troy," 88; "The Song of
  Wandering Aengus," 37, 92;
  "Who Goes with Fergus?" 36–
  37

About the Author

Patrick A. McCarthy, Professor of English at the University of Miami in Coral Gables, Florida, was educated at the University of Virginia and the University of Wisconsin-Milwaukee, where he received his Ph.D. in 1973. He has written two previous books, *The Riddles of "Finnegans Wake"* (Fairleigh Dickinson University Press, 1980) and *Olaf Stapledon* (Twayne, 1982), and well over two dozen articles. His recent articles on *Ulysses* include "Joyce's Unreliable Catechist: Mathematics and the Narration of 'Ithaca,' " in *ELH: A Journal of English Literary History;* "*Ulysses* and the Printed Page," in *Joyce's "Ulysses":* *The Larger Perspective;* and "Stuart Gilbert's *Ulysses,*" in *Classics of Joyce Criticism.* He has edited *Critical Essays on Samuel Beckett* (G. K. Hall, 1986) and coedited *The Legacy of Olaf Stapledon: Critical Essays and an Unpublished Manuscript* (Greenwood Press, 1989), and he serves on the editorial board of *Science-Fiction Studies.* He and his wife, Kitty, live in Davie, Florida. They have three children, to whom this book is dedicated.